D0060472

The Arena of PRAYER

LEARN THE SECRETS

OF THE WORLD'S

GREATEST PRIVILEGE—

PRAYER

BEN JENNINGS

The Arena of Prayer

Published by
New*Life* Publications
A ministry of Campus Crusade for Christ
375 Highway 74 South, Suite A
Peachtree City, GA 30269

Edited by Beth Lueders and Joette Whims

Design and production by Genesis Publications

Cover by Larry Smith & Associates

Printed in the United States of America.

Library of Congress Cataloging-in-Publication Data

Jennings, Ben A.
    The arena of prayer : learn the secrets of the world's greatest privilege—
prayer / by Ben Jennings.
      p. cm.
    Includes bibliographical references.
    ISBN 1-56399-131-4
    1. Prayer—Christianity. I. Title.

BV210.2 .J458 1999
248 3'2—dc21

                  99-047877

- Neighbor Jim Wunder, who generously gave me crucial computer assistance for headers, footnotes, graphics, and pagination as I typed the draft.

- Dr. Joe Kilpatrick, who came to the kingdom for such a time as this. Director of *NewLife* Publications, he gave invaluable counsel and placed marvelous editing and publishing resources at my disposal.

- Much credit and thanks go to Beth Lueders and Joette Whims, who spent long hours and days editing this book. Their timely suggestions and advice will never be forgotten.

- To the goodly number of friends who have literally prayed this book into being.

Acknowledgments

THIS BOOK HAS BEEN like a San Francisco cable car ride. Like the cable that pulls the car, the Lord has taken me on a magnificent ride through hilly streets to a gratifying destination. He began by giving me a growing urge: "Don't hoard the truths I have given you. Write them! Share them with people you may never meet."

My thanks to a host of people in Campus Crusade prayer conferences. They have represented 111 countries. God has used their responses to enlarge my own sense of urgency.

Special encouragers have included:

- My beloved wife of 52 years, Mary Jean. She allowed important task delays, prayed, bought needed equipment, arranged our travel schedules, took care of family finances, and spent many evenings alone while I worked on the computer.

- Dr. William R. Bright, founder and president of Campus Crusade for Christ. He is a marvelous role model in prayer and faith for me. His friendship and gracious foreword to this book are similar to a propeller to a ship. I am grateful.

- E. Bailey Marks, Campus Crusade's International Vice-President. His perspective, enthusiasm, faith, skill, and optimism continue to fuel the fire in my bones.

- Gene and Janis Cherry, a Priscilla and Aquila to me when I needed undisturbed time. They lent me their home in Hawaii for one month to pray and work on the text.

- Our daughter, Colleen Fraioli, a successful writer herself. Colleen set aside time from her own writing to review and give vitalizing communication counsel.

Contents

Scripture quotations designated Message are from *The Message*, © 1993 by Eugene H. Peterson.

Scripture quotations designated TLB are from *The Living Bible*, © 1971 by Tyndale House Publishers, Wheaton, Illinois.

For more information, write:

Australia Campus Crusade for Christ—P.O. Box 40, Flemington Markets, NSW 2129, Australia

Campus Crusade for Christ of Canada—Box 529, Sumas, WA 98295, USA

Campus Crusade for Christ—Agape, Fairgate House, King's Road, Tyseley, Birmingham, B11 2AA, United Kingdom

Lay Institute for Evangelism, Campus Crusade for Christ—P.O. Box 8786, Auckland, 1035, New Zealand

Campus Crusade for Christ—9 Lock Road #03-03, Paccan Centre, Singapore 108937

Great Commission Movement of Nigeria—P.O. Box 500, Fudaya Village, Bauchi Ring Road, Jos, Plateau State, Nigeria, West Africa

Campus Crusade for Christ International—100 Lake Hart Drive, Orlando, FL 32832-0100, USA

Foreword

THROUGH THE YEARS on different occasions, I have been invited to the White House to meet with the most powerful person on earth—the president of the United States. I have met with several of our presidents and with various heads of state in my many travels.

These have all been meaningful and memorable experiences. However, there is one invitation, one meeting that immeasurably transcends all such experiences combined. That is the invitation to meet with the Creator of the universe, the King of kings and Lord of lords.

I meet with Him many times each day. I do not need an appointment. I do not need to go through a secretary. At any moment of the day or night, you or I can meet with Him. He is always happy to hear from us. He even invites us to come "boldly" before His throne, an indescribable privilege purchased for us at Calvary by the precious blood of our Lord Jesus Christ (Hebrews 4:16). We come to Him in prayer by faith because, as Hebrews 11:6 records, we know that faith pleases Him.

Surely, this invitation from the Creator is the greatest privilege a person can ever experience. It is an offer to spend time with Him, to talk to Him, and to experience His love for us. He invites us to "hear" Him speak to us through His Word, the Bible, and through that still, small voice of the Holy Spirit. God draws us near to Him so that the reality of His presence is with us at all times. Our conversation with God is called prayer.

Prayer is so simple. Yet, deep principles of prayer and golden nuggets of wisdom are learned over time by committed saints on callused knees. These men and women, called by God to be intercessors, spend many hours in prayer closets communing with Him.

My dear friend Dr. Ben Jennings is one of those saints, and I am deeply honored to commend his book to you. This is a marvelous, inspiring, and helpful book on prayer. It is profoundly spiritual, yet down to earth. Every page will grip your attention and build your spirit.

Ben Jennings has been my close friend and fellow laborer in Christ for many years. Few people are as qualified to write such a book. God has called Ben to a ministry of prayer. He has been in the school of prayer for many years, has great maturity and experience in the things of the Lord, and has been a tireless prayer warrior at our Lord's feet for so long. Ben is a faithful, much loved servant of our Lord who has touched the lives of multitudes on every continent.

With this one book, Ben will take you by the hand and lead you down paths of wonderful insight that took him years to tread. I believe God will use this book, in a short time, to impart to you the wisdom the Lord has taught Ben through the deep experiences and lessons of a lifetime of service.

As you read, grasp, and apply the biblical truths in these pages, your prayer life will be enhanced and empowered, prayer answers will become more apparent, and demonic strongholds will crumble. As a result, more people will come into God's kingdom and the fulfillment of the Great Commission will be accelerated. Through all this, God will be glorified and, in a greater and more powerful way, His will done on earth as it is in heaven.

What could be greater? Join Ben and learn the secrets of the world's greatest privilege—prayer. You will never be the same!

DR. BILL BRIGHT
Founder and President
Campus Crusade for Christ International

CHAPTER 1

Prayer and Our Endangered WORLD

AROUND 1942, the Bamboo Curtain descended on China, beginning a new era of communist Chinese life. At that time, Protestant Christians numbered less than a million. The new dictator, Mao Tse-tung, unleashed an inferno of persecution on religion. Christians were martyred, churches confiscated, pastors imprisoned, and Bibles and hymnals destroyed.

Thousands of Christian believers began to meet in secret house churches across the land. For security reasons, prayer was the main activity possible for these harassed believers. As a result, Chinese Christians developed rapidly as a praying people. Missionaries expelled from China also united in a worldwide prayer team. One of them, Will Shubert, spoke in the chapel of Pacific Bible College (now Azusa Pacific University) where I was a student.

Shubert stated that he was dedicating himself to prayer for China. Six months later he returned to say, "I have *prayed through* for China." God had assured Shubert that He had heard his prayers and that He would complete His work in this largest of nations.

During the news blackout over the next thirty years, hints of tremendous church growth leaked out of China. An early report estimated that the number of Christians had doubled to 2 million. Years later rumor suggested that China might have as many as 8 million believers. China watchers dismissed this idea as ridiculous.

In 1984, Jonathan Chao, a China researcher, spoke to our tour group in Hong Kong. His staff had completed a province-by-province count of evangelical believers. They discovered that the church had grown—not to 2 million or 8 million people—but to 50 million!

Chao himself was broadcasting weekly seminary classes via radio to 1 million young pastors inside China. These men were in-service trainees leading this incredible underground church.

Three years later, I met one of Chao's board members in Malaysia. I asked him if the figure of 50 million Christians had been confirmed. "Yes," he replied, "but the number is now 80 million."

China's spiritual awakening through prayer may be the number one story of the Church Age. A forty-year government effort to stamp out religion has fanned the flames of prayer. House churches in China dedicated to prayer continue to increase exponentially. What an amazing story! Starting from less than 1 million Christians in 1950, the Church grew to an estimated 80 million by 1987.[1] Singapore Christian officials found that an average of 31,000 people per day placed their faith in Christ during 1997 alone.[2] Millions more are joining the ranks of God's army at the close of the 20th century. And the Chinese church has a powerful missionary vision! I have seen their published intention to evangelize China without foreign personnel or money.

Why Is Prayer Accelerating?

Without a doubt, prayer is influencing the world! For more than fifty years prayer has played a vigorous role within developing nations. The exciting news today is that prayer is also exploding in developed countries, casting a spiritual sunrise across the Western world.

Three major trends seem to be driving this mighty spiritual upsurge. First, *prayer is growing because of a moral meltdown in Christian lands.* United States Senator James Inhofe (Oklahoma) said while speaking at the 1997 Fasting and Prayer Conference in Dallas, Texas: "We are in the greatest moral revolution in our nation's history. Evil conditions have driven more people to prayer than ever before."

Global problems, legislation, and military measures all indicate a desperate international need for intervention of some kind. Multitudes are seeking that intervention from God.

Second, *expanding interest in the supernatural is stimulating prayer.* Secular and religious communications about the supernatural are creating immense curiosity. Biblical prayer, which deals with the Creator and His spectacular universal action arena, beckons like a mountain range or the starry universe.

Christian believers are realizing the essential place of prayer in the spiritual arena. Prayer and theology both deal with God, but from different perspectives. Theology, like a telescope, views the distant stars of His qualities. Prayer, like a space vehicle, moves us among His qualities. Theology studies God and prayer engages Him. Both are adventuresome. Both are necessary.

Third, *prayer is growing as people see God's hand directing the history of the world.* God used prayer movements and revivals to shape the moral character of areas such as Europe and America. In the past two centuries, movements of prayer have deeply affected almost every continent. Today, more people are recognizing the importance of prayer in every facet of society in every corner of the globe.

Can My Prayers Make a Difference?

I am sure you will agree that God is working in China in a supernatural way. But perhaps you are wondering: *What about in my life and my small community? All I see around me are declining moral values and spiritual lethargy. What can one person do about a deteriorating culture?*

Let me explain your role with an analogy. If you have ever attended a professional football game, you walked into an arena of strategy, action, and conflict. Within this arena are two teams—and only one will win. All the plays are conducted within the yardage marked out on the field. The players, relying on the training and direction of their coach, strive for the goal.

In some ways, God's prayer arena resembles a football contest. God's arena is an unseen world of faith and action, much more powerful and effective than anything we could imagine. This unseen world is unlimited and encompasses the entire universe.

An amazing part of the contest being waged right now is that we, as believers, are strategic players, as long as we follow the training and direction given us by God! Through prayer, we can travel farther than the stars to the very center of power—the throne of our God. Though we may fear our opponents' craftiness, we know that our divine, loving, perfect God of the universe will win the contest.

You are called to play a strategic role, although at times it may be difficult. Young Christians are often intrigued by the awesome nature of prayer, but, strangely, disappointment often besets older ones. "I believe God answers prayer," said a weary traveler. "He just doesn't answer mine." Even Isaiah lamented, "Truly You are God, who hide Yourself" (Isaiah 45:15). All of us have experienced low times like these, yet we should not become discouraged and take ourselves out of the game.

God is searching for intercessors, and this search will affect entire nations. Read His words as written by the prophet Ezekiel:

> "I sought for a man among them who would make a wall, and stand in the gap before Me on behalf of the land, that I should not destroy it; but I found no one. Therefore I have poured out My indignation on them; I have consumed them with the fire of My wrath; and I have recompensed their deeds on their own heads," says the Lord God (Ezekiel 22:30,31).

Your prayer is needed as much for your world as Ezekiel's prayers were for his. God is looking for strategic players to enter His prayer arena to help change the course of history—one person at a time.

The Arena of God
The study of prayer is an adventure like no other. Wherever you are in your spiritual growth process, this book can help you gain enthusiasm and comfort during times of discouragement, enlarge your vision of what God can and will do through your prayers, and help you determine God's calling for you in prayer—locally and worldwide.

Exploring God's arena through a series of Bible adventures, we will discover answers to many questions regarding the panorama of prayer. These questions include:

- Why did God create prayer?

- Where is the prayer arena of God and what is it like?
- How does God work in our world? What does He do and what does He expect of me?
- How can prayer increase to saturate an entire nation?
- What happens in heaven when people pray on earth?
- How does prayer relate to demons and Satan?
- Why do my prayers seem powerless?

Along with understanding the cosmic nature of prayer, we need to grasp its significance to us personally. Therefore, this book will also answer everyday questions like these:

- Prayer is often boring for me. How can it become exciting?
- My faith at times is weak. How can I grow strong in faith?
- Why doesn't God answer more of my prayers?

This study of prayer is designed for practical journeys into God's arena. Prayer is both taught and "caught." Without its biblical principles being taught, prayer is unstable. Without our "catching" the principles by applying them to our lives, it is sterile. Each chapter, therefore, provides teaching on the nature and realm of prayer and shows you steps to enlarge your prayer life. To help you better apply prayer dynamics to your individual life and within prayer groups, each chapter concludes with three personal features: a suggested Prayer Response for talking with God in bold, new ways, Personal Reflection questions, and a Practical Step for you to take.

The following is an overview of the sections of this book.

- *Part 1: Exploring God's Cosmic Panorama of Prayer*—In this section, we will learn about the cosmic war being waged around us. We will examine the scope, purpose, and future of prayer. We will explore motivations for developing a passionate prayer life.

- *Part 2: Action in God's Arena of Prayer*—This section discusses the roles of the essential figures in the celestial prayer circuit: the Father, the Son, the Holy Spirit, and each child of God. God the Father initiates prayer. God the Holy Spirit communicates prayer to us by entrusting concerns to our hearts. God the Son, our non-stop Mediator, brings answers to pass. God's praying people provide an astonishing, critical prayer connection in the process.

- *Part 3: Living in God's Prayer Arena*—Here we tackle the dilemma of reconciling communication between a perfect God and His faulty people. How can we approach Him? Do we dare look Him in the face? Can a person like me actually enjoy His holiness, develop mountain-moving faith, and win battles against Satan?

- *Part 4: Advancing in the Arena of Prayer*—In this part, we will look at ways to grow strong in the Lord through prayer. These chapters offer tools and encouragement for viewing and helping fulfill God's world plan. Whether you are just beginning a ministry of prayer, are involved in lay leadership, or lead a church or ministry, these concepts and resources can revitalize your praying.

- *Part 5: Resource Handbook for Fortifying Your Prayer*—Some of the chapters recommend worksheets and other practical material that will help you enlarge your prayer life. These resources are located in the Resource section for your convenience. Use the Resources like a handbook of ideas on prayer.

Taking the First Step
As you begin your reading, you will face a pivotal question: Am I willing to join a stream of explorers who have blazed trailways for the Lord in prayer? The following poem eloquently presents the urgency of this prayer commitment.

The Difference
I got up early one morning
and rushed right into the day;
I had so much to accomplish
that I didn't have time to pray.

Problems just tumbled about me,
and heavier came each task.
"Why doesn't God help me?" I wondered.
He answered, "You didn't ask."

I wanted to see joy and beauty,
but the day toiled on, gray and bleak;

I wondered why God didn't show me.
He said, "But you didn't seek."

I tried to come into God's presence;
I used all my keys at the lock.
God gently and lovingly chided,
"My child, you didn't knock."

I woke up early this morning,
and paused before entering the day;
I had so much to accomplish
that I had to take time to pray.

—*Author unknown*

A "yes" answer to the question above will help you enrich your adventure in the arena of prayer. The Bible is your foundation for the journey. Acts 17:11 records that Berean Christians "received the word with all readiness, and searched the Scriptures daily." Prayer grows in proportion to its grounding in God's Word. For this reason, all concepts in this book are rooted in Scripture. Many Scripture verses are listed so that you can use this book as a personal Bible study on prayer, for group studies, and even sermon outlines. Like the Berean Christians, search each Scripture reference for biblical instruction.

Will you join me in prayer as we open these pages? When you finish your prayer, carefully answer the Personal Reflection questions and complete the Practical Step to prepare your heart for Part 1.

Prayer Response
Gracious Lord, use this study to renew my mind and my heart. Lukewarmness seeps into my soul. Contentment with Your blessings displaces my desire for You, the Blesser. Make my love for You like a living fire! Increase my appetite for "that good and acceptable and perfect will of God" (Romans 12:2). Teach me to pray like You taught Your disciples (Luke 11:1). I truly want to learn. In your Son's holy name, amen.

Personal Reflection
- What kinds of things do you want to learn to become a prayer warrior?

- What life changes might you need to make?
- What situations do you have in which you need to ask God to strengthen your prayer life?

Practical Step
Have you observed that prayer is increasing in your part of the world? What are these evidences? Write down the changes you have seen over the past few months, years, or even decades. Also note causes that might have sparked these prayer movements.

PART ONE

Exploring God's Cosmic Panorama of PRAYER

Almost every person has some knowledge about prayer; and there are many people who would like to pray, but who sense the fact that they have no access to God. To the true Christian, however, prayer is life's highest and holiest privilege and greatest delight.

Theodore H. Epp, *Praying With Authority*

CHAPTER 2

Encountering the
SUPERNATURAL

GOD'S PANORAMA of prayer exists in a cosmic supernatural realm. My exploration of this realm began in India, an immense country full of mystery. An international group I served met in Bangalore a few years ago. Two friends, Norm Lewis and Sherman Williams, and I took the occasion to travel across Asia. Four scenes in that journey left lasting impressions on me.

Scene 1: Northern India

First, we visited northern India where 10 to 12 million Muslim people are loyal to the death for their faith. Mosques and minarets pepper the landscape. *What creates such extreme devotion to this religion?* we wondered.

An answer came through a question from national church planters near India's east coast. "What do you have to help us in casting out demons?" they asked.

"What do you mean?" I replied.

"When we go into a village, the first problem we face is demon possession. It is very difficult. Can you help us?"

At the time, I was serving at the United States Center for World Mission.[1] The purpose of the Center is to focus Christian attention on the world's hidden peoples—cultures beyond present missionary plans. The Center encountered satanic activity while buying a college campus in Pasadena, California. God used our prayers to remove a cult that was renting some of the buildings. But we had not yet

21

worked a study of demons into our curriculum.

Poorly versed in demon activity, I hesitantly answered the Indian pastors, "We leave that issue to each mission field." They received my answer politely, but their question traveled south with me and helped me begin to probe one of India's great mysteries.

Scene 2: Southern India

In southern India, Hindu temples—tiny and huge, covered with grotesque god-figures—are everywhere. Hindus worship 30 million gods. Despite widespread, severe poverty, Hindus display a religious passion which rivals that of the Muslims.

Again we wondered, *What is there about this religion that imprisons masses of people in such intense devotion?* A more complete answer was waiting a few days later across the Indian Ocean.

Scene 3: Singapore

A Hindu festival called Taipusam was under way in Singapore on Sunday, February 12. Men carried torture racks to repay their idols for answered prayers. The racks were made of curled metal strips and sacred peacock feathers. About fifty crisscross skewers, each perhaps twenty inches long, pierced the men's bare backs and chests. One skewer was also thrust through each man's cheeks and tongue. Yet there was no bleeding—no pain!

Surrounded by their clans, these men walked the two miles from one temple to another. At the second temple, they walked barefoot across a fire pit of red-hot coals, again without blisters or pain.

My host, a Chinese pastor, explained, "To prepare, these men spend two months praying in their temple to their gods." On this festival day they displayed a power beyond the human, the power of demons associated with their idols.

The Bible speaks of idol worship in 1 Corinthians 10:19,20: "What am I saying then? That an idol is anything, or what is offered to idols is anything? But I say that the things which the Gentiles [non-Jewish people] sacrifice they sacrifice to demons and not to God, and I do not want you to have fellowship with demons."

We were seeing firsthand that the *supernatural* element is the glue that cements millions of people to their religions. Demonic power was the agent in Islam that challenged the Christian church planters and also the power that ruled masses of Hindus. This common demonic thread ran through Buddhist lands as well.

Scene 4: Thailand

Gilded Buddhist temples are everywhere in Thailand. Millions of people pray to smiling Buddhas as well as fierce-looking idols. Colorful, doll-sized "spirit houses" stand in front of homes, restaurants, and offices. The people in Asia implore *demons* to live in these houses as their personal, family, or business spirit. Incredibly, they pray to demons to guide, protect, and favor them.

Fresh food and flowers are kept in each little house to keep the resident demon in a prayer-answering mood. Producing and selling these small shrines is a large industry.

Prayer and Spiritual Warfare

One night in Bangkok, Thailand, sleep fled from me and I didn't feel well. Images from previous days, especially the Hindu torture procession, churned in my mind. Evil spirits were ruling oceans of Asian people. Jesus seemed very small in that setting.

I prayed into the night, *Lord, how can this be? You disabled Satan two thousand years ago on the cross. You, Yourself, declared, "Now is the judgment of this world; now the ruler of this world will be cast out. And I, if I am lifted up from the earth, will draw all peoples to Myself"* (John 12:31,32). *How is it possible that demons still hold these masses in captivity?*

I sensed His reply, "Ben, I did break Satan's power in My death and resurrection. You are seeing areas in which My victory has not yet been applied by prayer. Great intercessors have lived and served here—saints like Amy Carmichael, John 'Praying' Hyde, and Adoniram Judson. But a few people alone cannot cover millions."

In the darkness of that night, Ephesians 6:10–12 came to my mind:

> Finally, my brethren, be strong in the Lord and in the power of His might. Put on the whole armor of God, that you may be able to stand against the wiles [schemes] of the devil. For we do not wrestle against flesh and blood, but against principalities, against powers, against the rulers of the darkness of this age,

against spiritual hosts of wickedness in the heavenly places.

The verses struck deep. *Lord, You are calling us to war! You order us to attack evil forces that besiege the human realm. But why would You lead us into this kind of a conflict? We are hopelessly outclassed.*

Then I was drawn to verse 18 in that same chapter. Amazingly, God gives us prayer to deal with these supernatural domains: "Praying always with all prayer and supplication in the Spirit, being watchful to this end with all perseverance and supplication for all the saints."

"Praying" in that verse is a participle, not an imperative. A participle gathers up related information and places it in an action mode.

Let me explain with an example: When *traveling* (a participle) to Mexico City, *visit* some Mayan ruins, *taste* some delicious oranges, and *fish* for some marlin (all imperatives). The participle, "traveling," provides a setting for the instructions to "visit," "taste," and "fish."

In the same way, the passage we just looked at, Ephesians 6:10–18, contains three instructions: *Be strong in the Lord* (verse 10). *Put on the whole armor of God* (verses 11,13). *Battle Satan's hierarchy* (verse 12).

"Praying" in verse 18 provides an avenue to express these actions. "Praying" describes *how* to be strong in the Lord, *how* to put on His armor, and *how* to tackle evil. Prayer is a super-weapon!

Reviewing those Asian scenes in my room that night, I became angry. Jesus Christ forever defeated Satan at Calvary. Christians can connect His victory to Satan's strongholds and bring deliverance to captives throughout the world. But millions of beautiful people before my very eyes in Asia had not been released to our God.

Where are the intercessors? This cannot go on! my soul cried out to God. That night I dedicated my life to God for mobilizing spiritual warfare through international prayer. When I returned home, my wife, Mary Jean, readily joined me in that decision. Today we are experiencing Jesus' promise as given in John 10:4, "When he brings out his own sheep, he goes before them; and the sheep follow him, for they know his voice." Where He guides, He provides.

The first step Mary Jean and I took was to begin development of an institute for prayer at the United States Center for World Mission (initially named the Andrew Murray Institute after the famed South African leader). The following year, Campus Crusade for Christ invited Mary Jean and me to lead prayer development in 150 countries served by the ministry at that time.[2] Prayer coordinators now lead the ministry's prayer branch, the Great Commission Prayer Movement (GCPM), in fourteen continental areas and 172 countries.

Principals for Worldwide Prayer

Prayers give God ports of entry into human affairs. More intercessors provide more avenues for God to work. As we intercede in prayer, we can call forth God's action anywhere. The China story in Chapter 1 illustrated prayer-power worldwide. It relates principles of prayer for Christians of all nations. These principles include:

1. Prayer is God's way for people to digest His Word. Years of exposure to the Bible are a seedbed for movements of prayer.

2. God motivates us to pray by drawing us close to Him alone. God often uses circumstances to turn us toward prayer. The expulsion of missionaries from China precipitated the prayer that led to the explosive growth in the Chinese church.

3. Prayer produces revival among Christians, even under difficult circumstances.

4. Prayer follows an ascending spiral. Praying individuals lead to praying churches. Praying churches produce more praying people, and so on.

5. As prayer completes a large sphere in which God does His work on earth, praying Christians multiply exponentially.

6. The spread of evangelism parallels the spread of prayer.

A new day is here for worldwide prayer. More and more prayer ministries are networking together around the globe to mobilize intercessors. When you pray, you are not alone. God is ready to use you, together with all of His intercessors, to complete His world plan. We can take direction from Jesus' Great Commission to His followers in Matthew 28:18–20:

> Jesus came and spoke to them, saying, "All authority has been given to Me in heaven and on earth. Go therefore and make dis-

ciples of all nations, baptizing them in the name of the Father and of the Son and of the Holy Spirit, teaching them to observe all things that I have commanded you; and lo, I am with you always, even to the end of the age."

He gives four "alls" to inflame our praying. *All authority* gives us access to total power in our prayers. *All nations* directs us to pray for every location on earth. *All commands* reminds us to equip ourselves with strategic training. *All time* reveals a current urgency for our prayers.

Today, Great Commission prayer—praying for the fulfillment of the Great Commission—is reaching far beyond all that we can ask or imagine (Ephesians 3:20). Four major indicators show that prayer is accelerating around the globe.

An estimated 85 million intercessors are at work. While a precise count of world intercessors is almost impossible, the AD2000 and Beyond Movement[3] estimates 50 million people taking part in specific prayer programs for the 10-40 Window (an area between the 10th and 40th parallels, extending from western Africa across Asia to the Pacific Ocean).

PrayUSA![4] estimates that each year 15 million people participate in month-long prayer for America. Of South Korea's 46 million people, nearly 30 percent are Protestant, and most of these Christians are intercessors. With more than 80,000 missionaries in the world and each of them backed by a sizable number of prayer supporters, 85 million intercessors worldwide seems like a reasonable count.

Second, *more nations than ever have become open to the gospel.* In 1993, missiologist Patrick Johnstone reported that 35 new countries opened to Christian workers over the past thirty years. These doors, he said, were dramatically opened in answer to prayer.[5]

Third, *the good news of Christ is penetrating closed regions.* Specific information on these areas cannot be published for security reasons, but we can rejoice in knowing that the gospel is going extensively into nations long resistant to Christianity.

Fourth, *several organizations are publishing entire catalogs about prayer movements.*[6] The Christian Information Network is in touch with well over 50 million international praying people. Campus Crusade for Christ is compiling a roster scheduled to include all nations.

As God calls us to intercession, we need not be afraid. Intercessors are part of a huge, growing army battling in a cosmic setting. In the next chapter, we will begin exploring the arena of prayer by discovering God's theater of operations. Other areas we will cover will be our training to reign with Christ, the incredible power God releases through our prayers, and the decisive turning point in the war against evil powers that assures us victory.

God's arena is fascinating and exciting. We gain much confidence in prayer by observing how God's master plan will accomplish all He promises—and more!

Prayer Response

Gracious Father, evil powers frighten me. I hesitate to confront them in prayer. Forgive me for underestimating You. You are far greater than Satan. Teach me how to merge my prayers with Your power. Through Jesus Christ I pray. Amen.

Personal Reflection

- What one concern do you have that you feel is too big for prayer? What is there about this concern that worries you?

- What spiritual battles have you fought recently?

- What spiritual weapons did you use? (See Ephesians 6:12–18.)

Practical Step

Make a chart with three columns. In the first column, list the problems you are experiencing in your prayer life. In the second column, list how you think this study will be helpful to you for each problem. When you finish this book, review your answers. Then in the third column, write how you will address these problems.

CHAPTER 3

God's Theater of OPERATIONS

C AN YOU IMAGINE trying to pack the sun into a AAA battery case? Ludicrous! Solar energy is so intense that we cannot even come near to the sun.

Prayer also has so much power that we cannot measure or contain it. That's because the power of prayer is directly related to the power of God. And God's power is greater than we could ever imagine.

Our prayer power is related to how valuable God considers our communication with Him. He longs to hear from us. God's desire to communicate with us is illustrated in His goodness. You do not have a single benefit that did not come from God. James writes that He is "the Father of lights" (James 1:17). He grants each answer to prayer just like He causes the sun, moon, and stars to continually shine. Sometimes you cannot see those heavenly bodies, but they never stop shining. In a similar way, His answering never stops.

Our confidence in prayer comes from the fact that prayer is shaped by the nature of God. The apostle John writes, "We love Him because He first loved us" (1 John 4:19). In other words, we love Him in response to His love. In a similar way, we crave to pray because He has a craving for our prayers.

Therefore, to truly understand God's purpose and action in prayer, we must begin by understanding His nature. Because of His complexity and unlimited, eternal qualities, we cannot fathom the depths of His character. Yet, we can grasp what God has revealed to us about Himself in His Word. These facts about God are essential to our praying with authority and purposefulness. Knowing Him allows us to pray correctly—and with assurance.

God exists in three Persons: Father, Son, and Holy Spirit. When we pray, however, we do not pray to three Gods. We worship *one* God in three Persons. Like a circle, God's unity is complete and unbroken. We cannot say, "Here is this part of God, and over there is another part of God." All of God is everywhere.

God's plural oneness is called the Trinity, or a tri-unity. This tri-unity is so strong that Scriptures speak of the three as "He." For example, a plural name for God is often used with singular-person action words: "In the beginning God [*Elohim*, plural] created [*barah*, singular] the heavens and the earth" (Genesis 1:1).

God's threefold existence is pictured in Christ's Great Commission: "baptizing them in the name [singular] of the Father and of the Son and of the Holy Spirit" (Matthew 28:19). Each of the three Persons of the Trinity carries a distinct role in prayer. The Bible teaches us to pray to the Father (Matthew 6:9), in Jesus' name (John 16:24), relying on the guidance and enabling of the Holy Spirit (Romans 8:26). In fact, prayer helps us better understand God's threefold nature.

Because people don't realize the strength of God's character and His desire for them to interact with Him, they often consider prayer a tiny action in daily life. They try to compress it into a spare second or two, like putting the sun into a battery case. Then they wonder why their prayers are ineffective. They don't realize that prayer catapults us far beyond anything we can see and into God's theater of operations.

Prayer is limitless because God is limitless. Prayer is alive because God is alive. Prayer is powerful because God has total power. Prayer results begin immediately because God is timeless. When you pray, you align yourself with God and His purposes. Prayer propels you to your highest possible potential.

David was awed by his privilege of talking with God. He declared, "When I consider Your heavens, the work of Your fingers, the moon and the stars, which You have ordained, what is man that You are mindful of him, and the son of man that You visit him? For

You have made him a little lower than the angels, and You have crowned him with glory and honor" (Psalm 8:3–5).

St. Augustine, a fourth-century church father, also revered communion with God when he prayed, "Thou has made us for Thyself, O God; and our hearts are restless until they find their rest in Thee."[1] We have all experienced that feeling of discontent when we fail to communicate with our Maker and heavenly Father. But we feel such joy when we are able to touch the sphere of our eternal Father!

The Panorama of Prayer

Prayer cannot be confined to our finite world. It deals with a Creator who is greater than all the starry heavens. Prayer launches people into the limitless, powerful arena of God Himself. The apostle Paul, a mighty prayer warrior himself, places prayer in a cosmic setting in Romans 8:26,27:

> Likewise the Spirit also joins in to help our weakness. For we do not know what we should pray for as is necessary, but the Spirit Himself makes intercession for us with unexpressed groanings. But the One who searches the hearts knows what the mind of the Spirit is, because He [the heart-searcher] intercedes on behalf of saints according to God.[2]

These verses are reference points—what I call the key verses—for the chapters that follow. They tie prayer to the nature of God, then add the human factor—His people. Our key verses paint an awesome picture of prayer. They present Spirit-directed prayer as taking place in the huge sphere of God's action, as pictured in the diagram on the following page. (Note that the graphic serves as a *functional* diagram only. It does not indicate three Gods, but merely shows the separate *actions* that each Person of the Trinity carries out in prayer.) The circle represents the total mutual harmony of God's triple action in prayer. The major players in the cosmic arena of prayer are located at the four quadrants of the circle.

At the zenith is God the Father to whom prayer is rightly directed. Prayer is heard in heaven when it is offered "according to God" (verse 27). Prayer flows *from* the Father and also *to* Him. Intercessors not only talk to the heavenly Father, but they listen as well.

Our Heavenly Father

Jesus Christ

THE NATURE

OF

PRAYER

Holy Spirit

Christian

One of Jesus' first prayer lessons for His disciples shows this two-way action: "But you, when you pray, go into your room, and when you have shut your door, pray to your Father who is in the secret place; and your Father who sees in secret will reward you openly" (Matthew 6:6).

Our key verses mention three intercessors who are located at the other quadrants of the prayer circle. All three are essential players.

The first intercessor mentioned, at the lowly six o'clock position, is the praying Christian. People are mentioned first. Why is our praying important? After all, in verse 26 the first thing said about our praying is that "we do not know what we should pray for as is necessary." For answers, we must look at the next two intercessors.

The second intercessor at three o'clock is the Holy Spirit. He intercedes for the fulfillment of God's world plan with longings that are, literally, not expressed. He carries out His praying within your life as a Christian believer. Amazingly, our prayers provide expression for the groanings of the Holy Spirit!

A third intercessor is situated at nine o'clock. The verse does not give His name, but describes His operation—He searches the hearts of praying people and prays for them according to God. Who is this person? We can determine His identity through His actions—searching the hearts of praying people.

There is nothing new about God searching human hearts. He has done that for centuries. David, for example, prayed, "Search me, O God, and know my heart; try me, and know my anxieties; and see if there is any wicked way in me, and lead me in the way everlasting" (Psalm 139:23,24). A reference in the New Testament, however, identifies one specific Person in the Trinity who has this responsibility. Revelation 2:18,23 names Him as the Son of God— our Lord Jesus Christ. "These things says the Son of God, who has eyes like a flame of fire...'All the churches shall know that I am He who searches the minds and hearts.'"

Romans 8:34 confirms the intercessory role of Jesus. "It is Christ who died, and furthermore is also risen, who is even at the right hand of God, who also makes intercession for us."

A dramatic scenario thus comes to light in these key verses. God the Father unfolds His redemptive plan for the world. God the Holy Spirit receives each part of that plan as an intense longing or "groaning." He communicates these longings to poorly praying Christians and helps them to pray better. God, the searching Son, receives those longings in the prayers of His people. The Son, the Lord Jesus, then presents those prayers back to the Father and sees that they get answered.

Author S. D. Gordon describes this circuit of prayer as an "unbroken circuit between the throne and the footstool, and God's desires were only flowing through us and returning to Himself again."[3]

In this way, the circuit of God's action is completed in the world. This is the way in which God is effecting His will and restoring His kingdom to a rebel society (Matthew 6:10).

What Happens When I Pray?

Picture a lonely Christian battered by a barrage of painful conditions. In desperation, he steps into his prayer closet and brings his battle into the heavenly realm. As he kneels in that little corner, something happens that is more powerful than earthquakes or hurricanes. His prayer, offered with a small, weak voice, engages action that reverberates through the universe!

Even when this pray-er has little strength left, his mere thoughts in prayer to his heavenly Father are just what God is waiting for. The

Trinity, in total unity, wisdom, and power, takes that heartfelt cry to God and transforms it into action within God's theater of operations.

Can you relate your prayers to this scene? Do you see them as part of God's cosmic panorama? Can you sense the power of God's promise? Can you regard the prayers of the saints as something precious to Him (Revelation 5:8)?

Our key verses in Romans 8:26,27 inspire seven conclusions about the role of prayer in God's arena:

- Prayer is more than something you do; it is something God does through you.
- Prayer completes the circuit of God's action in the world.
- Prayer does not change God's will, it effects His will.
- When you pray, you step into the operation of the Trinity.
- The significant part of your prayer is the praying of the Holy Spirit; your prayer is a primary way through which the Spirit prays.
- The powerful part of your prayer is the praying of Christ; your prayer is the main material for which Jesus is praying.
- Praying makes your Christian life supernatural; God gets His work done through your praying.

Hudson Taylor gives this insight regarding our prayer: "I used to ask God to help me. Then I asked if I might help Him. I ended up by asking Him to do His work through me."[4] Praying Christians are not powerful people. Their prayers are simply the conduit through which their powerful God lifts them from the human realm into His supernatural sphere.

God shows tremendous love to us by including our prayers in His action arena. He took extreme measures to make our praying possible. John 14:26 encourages us to remember that the Holy Spirit is our teacher and that He is helping us understand the cosmic nature of prayer. God has granted immense potential to you in prayer. He designed your prayer as an active connection for Him to your world.

The Problem of Prayerlessness
Considering the limitless nature of prayer, we also can visualize the serious nature of prayerlessness. Prayerlessness is an insult to God.

Every prayerless day is a statement by a helpless individual, "I do not need God today." Failing to pray reflects idolatry—a trust in substitutes for God. We rely on our money instead of God's provision. We rest on our own flawed thinking rather than on God's perfect wisdom. We take charge of our lives rather than trusting God. We consider His arena to be trivial until crushing needs drive us to our knees in prayer.

Prayerlessness short-circuits the working of God. In His love, He imposes Himself on no one. He waits to be asked. Neglecting prayer, therefore, is not a weakness; it is a sinful choice. Thank God that the atoning blood of Christ Jesus can remove the guilt of the sin of prayerlessness, for His blood cleanses the believer from all sin.

Perhaps you are thinking, *I would love to have a powerful prayer life, but I just can't seem to make it happen. Every time I try, something comes up and I fail.*

There is hope for prayerlessness! The Spirit of God can change a weak and deficient prayer life into one that is powerful and effective, but four actions are necessary. Eagerly take these four steps before proceeding with this book.

1. *Be sure that you are a Christian.* If you have any doubt about Christ living in you or that you are a member of God's family, please turn to Appendix A, "Knowing God Personally." Read thoughtfully through the material, then pray a prayer like the one suggested to invite Jesus into your life. Notice His guarantees on the pages that follow. Your prayer of invitation begins a life of prayer, and prayer literally becomes your lifeline.

2. *Repent of prayerlessness which dishonors your God.* Every significant life decision starts with a changed heart. Admit how weak, wayward, and insufficient you are. Ask God now to cleanse you of your wrong attitudes toward prayer and to fill you with a desire to communicate with Him continuously.

3. *Be filled with the Holy Spirit,* as commanded in Ephesians 5:18. The Holy Spirit is the Spirit of prayer (Zechariah 12:10). If you are not familiar with the concept of being filled with the Spirit, read *Have You Made the Wonderful Discovery of the Spirit-Filled Life?* (published by Campus Crusade for Christ). It will give you

the steps to being filled with the Holy Spirit. Then ask God to
fill you as He promises He will.

4. *Commit to center your schedule on daily time for you to meet God in
   prayer.* We make time for the things we consider important. Your
   daily routine reveals what those things are for you. Make prayer
   the first priority in your day. Schedule it as your most pressing
   business appointment. Keep that appointment with God.

Exploring God's arena takes us to the action in the heavens. In
our next chapter, we will glimpse things going on in that awesome
realm!

Prayer Response

*My God, You stoop to accomplish Your will through the prayers of people
like me. This is marvelous! I long to know more about that. I confess my
ignorance and low regard for prayer. Forgive me in Your great mercy.
Fill me with Your Holy Spirit. I want to give myself as a willing servant
to fit into Your plan and to center my life around communion with You.
In the name of Jesus, amen.*

Personal Reflection

- What part of praying is most impressive to you? Why?
- What practical ways can we attract other people into the prayer
  arena?
- How would you express Psalm 116:1,2 in your own words?
- What keeps you from setting and keeping a daily time of prayer?

Practical Step

Use the four steps on the preceding page to evaluate your priorities
in prayer. As you give prayer first priority for the next week, write
down the changes that occur in your life. At the end of the week, jot
down a number of differences you find in your communion with
God. Thank God for the new closeness you enjoy with Him.

CHAPTER 4

The Cross and
COSMIC WAR

T HE BATTLE OF MIDWAY between the United States and Japan
turned the course of World War II. After a disastrous attack
on Pearl Harbor, the Japanese achieved one military success
after another. They struck Hong Kong, Singapore, the Philippines,
and Malaya, and were advancing toward Australia. The Japanese
Imperial Navy seemed unstoppable.

On the morning of June 4, 1942, Americans launched land- and
carrier-based attacks on the Japanese forces near the Midway Islands
in the Pacific Ocean. The Americans had three carrier ships; the
Japanese had four. The Japanese had superior naval power at their
disposal. Americans possessed radio and message-decoding advantages. Technology gave the Allied Forces a much better idea of the
opponent's size and whereabouts.

In five minutes of battle, the American dive-bomber pilots inflict-
ed severe damage to three of the Japanese carriers, giving the victory
to the Allied Forces. The Battle of Midway set a direction for battles
that followed.

A war between God and Satan started in the Garden of Eden. Its
decisive battle climaxed at Calvary—a turning point that is deter-
mining spiritual warfare today. (I use the term "Calvary" to represent
the full redemptive work of Christ—His death, burial, resurrection,
and ascension.)

In Colossians 2:15, Paul describes the triumph of this turning-

37

point battle: "Having disarmed the powers and authorities, [Jesus] made a public spectacle of them, triumphing over them by the cross" (NIV). Unlike the Battle of Midway, Christ's victory was complete and once-for-all. What at first seemed like the defeat of the ages—the death of God's Messiah—became the supreme moment of history!

How Did Spiritual Warfare Begin?

You remember the story of the beginning of the human race. Our first parents disobeyed God in the Garden of Eden. Adam and Eve ate of the tree of the knowledge of good and evil. What was so bad about that? Romans 5:12 explains:

> Therefore, just as through one man sin entered the world, and death through sin, and thus death spread to all men, because all sinned.

How could that one act plunge the entire human race into total sin and death? Here is what happened.

When God created Adam and Eve, He delegated world dominion to them (Genesis 1:26–28). They became world emperors under God's authority. By yielding to Satan's plan, that first pair transferred their line of authority from God to Satan, and made Satan the ruler of this world (John 12:31).

The disobedience of Adam reaped the kind of world we live in today—a world of sin, depravity, curse, and death. No human solution has ever been found.

Immediately after Eden, the Father launched an amazing strategy. The problem was that Satan's captives had themselves chosen him to be their king. They were prisoners by their own choice.

God had anticipated these developments. Before Creation, He made plans to invade the rebel kingdom, rescue His people, and change their hostile character. God would Himself confront the enemy, allow Satan to hit Him with all the weapons in his arsenal, destroy all of Satan's artillery, and liberate His people forever.

The Battle of All Time

The plan unfolded when God came to earth in the form of an infant. An angel announced the baby's mission to Joseph, "You shall call His name Jesus, for He will save His people from their sins"

(Matthew 1:21). Because Jesus was born of a virgin, He did not inherit man's sinful, spiritually dead nature. This Jesus lived a perfectly pure life with no trace of sin.

This same Jesus went voluntarily to execution as a substitute for all sinners. He could do so because He is God and without sin. *On a Roman cross, Jesus took into His body all the ammunition that Satan possessed and changed history forever.* The cross became the turning point of history in several ways:

- *Jesus became our sin—all that is evil in the world.* He voluntarily accepted everything that separated people from the Father, such as our rebellion (active and passive), egotism, idolatry, deception, and lust. (See Romans 1–3 for a more complete summary of sin.) Jesus *bore* all the sins of the world in His own body on the cross (1 John 2:2). He *became* our sin (2 Corinthians 5:21)! The pure, holy God-man drank all the cup of sin for all humanity for all time.

- *Jesus became our curse—all that is wrong in the world.* Sin condemned people and even nature. God decreed to Adam, "Because you have heeded the voice of your wife, and have eaten from the tree of which I commanded you, saying, 'You shall not eat of it': Cursed is the ground for your sake; in toil you shall eat of it all the days of your life. Both thorns and thistles it shall bring forth for you, and you shall eat the herb of the field. In the sweat of your face you shall eat bread till you return to the ground, for out of it you were taken; for dust you are, and to dust you shall return" (Genesis 3:17–19).

  Who could ever remove a curse like this from humankind? Paul explains in Galatians 3:13, "Christ has redeemed us from the curse of the law, having become a curse for us (for it is written, 'Cursed is everyone who hangs on a tree')."

- *Christ received death for everyone—all that is destructive in the world.* By becoming like us with a human body, Christ could and did receive a death sentence that redeemed our race. "Since the children are made of flesh and blood, it's logical that the Savior took on flesh and blood in order to rescue them by his death. By embracing death, taking it into himself, he destroyed the Devil's hold on death and freed all who cower through life, scared to death of death" (Hebrews 2:14,15, *The Message*).

- *When Jesus arose from the dead, He broke the power of everything that killed Him.* Included in the list of crushed enemies were sin ("Behold! The Lamb of God who takes away the sin of the world!"—John 1:29); death ("I am He who lives, and was dead, and behold, I am alive forevermore. Amen. And I have the keys of Hades and of Death"—Revelation 1:18); and the curse ("There shall be no more curse, but the throne of God and of the Lamb shall be in it, and His servants shall serve Him"—Revelation 22:3). That was the turning point of the war!

How Can Calvary Energize My Praying?

Christ's victory on Calvary not only allows us to have a relationship with God, but paved the way for us to communicate with our heavenly Father through prayer. Christ died and arose for three prayer purposes.

His death and resurrection created intercessors. "Christ also suffered once for sins, the just for the unjust, *that He might bring us to God,* being put to death in the flesh but made alive by the Spirit" (1 Peter 3:18). In Hebrews 11:6, the phrase "comes to God" refers to prayer, whether the prayer is someone's first or millionth.

His sacrifice and victory neutralized enemy opposition. Paul writes in Philippians 2:8–11, "Being found in appearance as a man, He humbled Himself and became obedient to the point of death, even the death of the cross. Therefore, God also has highly exalted Him and given Him the name which is above every name, that at the name of Jesus every knee should bow, of those in heaven, of those on earth, and of those under the earth, and that every tongue should confess that Jesus Christ is Lord, to the glory of God the Father." No believer in Christ Jesus is any longer a slave of sin and Satan. We belong to God! Our prayer is freely and fully accepted by the Father and has access to His greatness.

Christ's righteous act paid the cost for all answers to prayer. Now we can draw near to God, an action that sin disqualified before we received Jesus as our Savior. "Therefore, brethren, having boldness to enter the Holiest by the blood of Jesus, by a new and living way which He consecrated for us, through the veil, that is, His flesh, and having a High Priest over the house of God, let us draw near with a true heart in full assurance of faith, having our hearts sprinkled from an evil conscience and our bodies washed with pure water" (Hebrews 10:19–22).

Prayers flow worldwide from the victory of Calvary. The cross of Jesus was the turning point for prayer. When we pray in the name of Jesus, we pray with His authority over Satan. We hang our prayers on the power of Christ's resurrection.

The cross is God's master plan. The victory achieved on Calvary is so extensive that Jesus could say in Matthew 28:18, "All authority has been given to Me in heaven and on earth." No power in the universe can compare to His. Praying in His name means praying with His total power. Therefore, the cross is a wonderful seven-pillar foundation for our prayers.

1. *Christ displaced Satan's mastery over us.* Jesus declared, "'Now is the judgment of this world; now the ruler of this world will be cast out. And I, if I am lifted up from the earth, will draw all peoples to Myself.' This He said, signifying by what death He would die" (John 12:31–33).

2. *Jesus removed barriers to His holy fellowship.* "Who gave Himself for us, that He might redeem us from every lawless deed and purify for Himself His own special people, zealous for good works" (Titus 2:14).

3. *He gave His supreme authority to us.* "God was in Christ reconciling the world to Himself, not imputing their trespasses to them, and has committed to us the word of reconciliation" (2 Corinthians 5:19).

4. *He is providing His power for our praying.* "The weapons of our warfare are not carnal [of the flesh] but mighty in God for pulling down strongholds" (2 Corinthians 10:4).

5. *Jesus guarantees answers to our prayers.* "Whatever you ask the Father in My name He may give you" (John 15:16).

6. *He is giving us complete acceptance with God.* "He who did not spare His own Son, but delivered Him up for us all, how shall

He not with Him also freely give us all things?" (Romans 8:32).

7. *Christ's victory covers all time and situations.* "Thanks be to God who always leads us in triumph in Christ" (2 Corinthians 2:14).

Praying in Jesus' name means that He has given us power of attorney in His behalf. He backs the claims we bring to the Father in His name. His name carries His authority. You represent Jesus when you pray in His name. Intercessors connect Calvary to needs that God entrusts to them. We engage Christ's total supremacy to accomplish God's plan on earth.

Ephesians 1:19–23 explains the transfer of power that God has given to Christ and to us: "The exceeding greatness of [God's] power toward us who believe, according to the working of His mighty power which He worked in Christ when He raised Him from the dead and seated Him at His right hand in the heavenly places...And He put all things under His feet, and gave Him to be head over all things to the church, which is His body, the fullness of Him who fills all in all."

The exciting part of this cosmic war is that we are in a battle with a guaranteed victory. Our side has already won the war. Spiritual battles today are "mopping up" operations. We have an inside track on enemy moves because God knows everything. We have superior weapons because God is all-powerful. Prayer is the Armed Forces of Christ's Great Commission.

Military personnel are given extensive training for combat. Likewise, our Lord provides battle training for intercessors. He has a strategic plan for our prayer battles. In our next chapter, we will see how this training will set us up for a future that extends into eternity.

Prayer Response
I give glory to You, Christ Jesus, for the total victory and authority You have achieved. Demons and Satan himself are subject to Your name. You have overcome all opposition. And You invite me to use Your name when I pray! You guarantee answers with Your own supremacy! Oh, help me to utilize Your victory in my praying, for Your glory. I gratefully receive Your legacy and give myself to exercise the power of Your holy name. Amen.

Personal Reflection

- If you were God, would you have permitted Satan to continue his activity on earth? Why?

- Should people be overjoyed with the victory of Jesus at Calvary? Is this joy true of you?

- How might you more consistently enjoy the conquest of Calvary?

Practical Step

1. Write about an evil situation within your sphere of activity—your home, family, school, business, community, or even your church.

2. Bring that case to God in prayer, connecting it to the victory of Christ at Calvary.

3. Worship the Lord for one of His attributes. Choose one that relates to the problem at hand. (Refer to Appendix B for a list of God's attributes.) For example:

If Your Situation Is...	*Worship God for His...*
A disagreeable colleague	Peace
A sick friend	Care
A lonely feeling	Fatherhood

4. Sustain this prayer-worship connection daily until God lifts the burden from you and until you have "cast all your care upon Him" (1 Peter 5:7).

CHAPTER 5

Training for
REIGNING

D OES PRAYER EVER seem strange to you? You talk to Someone you cannot see. You listen for Someone you cannot hear. You ask for answers outside the human realm.

Our previous chapter described God's ultimate authority that makes your praying possible. We move now to a cosmic drama in Revelation that helps explain some mystery about prayer. Why did God create prayer? Follow the scenes in chapters 4 and 5 of that spectacular book.

In this story, the apostle John is an old man, probably in his nineties. He is called to heaven and sees a scene of sheer splendor. A gigantic throne encircled by an emerald-like rainbow captivates him. Lightning flashes; voices and thunder boom.

The Person on the throne is too dazzling to describe. "Earth and sky fled from His presence," John wrote later in Revelation 20:11 (NIV). His celestial throne makes it clear that He is God the Father.

White-robed elders with crowns of gold are seated on individual thrones around the throne of God. Their robes identify them as representatives of all God's people, for the white robes are the righteousness of the saints (Revelation 19:8,14).

Four living beings around the high throne appear to represent the angels of heaven (Revelation 4:6–9). They look very much like the beings described in Isaiah 6:2 and Ezekiel 1:5–28. Here are saints and angels worshiping God together. They never stop to rest.

Solving a Universal Dilemma

A sea of glass spreads out before the throne. Seven flaming lamps stand on the sea, reflecting brilliance into its depths and radiance in all directions. The right hand of the Father, however, is the main object of John's attention. God holds a scroll with seven seals.

The scroll appears to be the title deed to the universe. Each seal, as it is broken later, restores part of creation to God's control. In the scroll, John sees a coming climax to human destiny.

A mighty angel cries out, "Who is qualified to open the seals of the scroll?" That someone must be qualified to rescue humanity for God. That person must be free from the sin that has condemned the world. He needs to conquer the curse that enslaves creation and the death that dooms it.

A universal search begins (Revelation 5:2). There is no time to lose. The final hope of the world is in the balance. But alas, in all of creation—throughout the universe—absolutely no one is found.

The old apostle's heart breaks; he sobs in dismay (5:4). He has lived so long, suffered so much, and tried so hard to rescue people. But the satanic Roman Empire, not the kingdom of God, is controlling mankind.

Wait! An elder rises from his throne and comes near to the weeping patriarch. "Don't cry," he says. "It's not over! The Lion of Judah has been qualified to take possession of earth!"

John looks up, but sees no lion. Instead, through his tears he sees a mangled Lamb as if he had escaped from a slaughter house. The Lamb is standing at the throne of God. No wonder He was not found anywhere else in creation! Despite His deathly appearance, the Lamb comes forward, full of power (seven horns) and wisdom (seven eyes). He looks like a sacrifice but moves like a sovereign. He is our Lord Jesus Christ!

He takes the scroll, and the hosts of heaven and earth break forth in galactic jubilee. They fall before the Lamb in adoration and praise. The largest celebration ever recorded begins. Voices of angels and saints explode in vast choral adoration. They sing with harps and carry gold bowls filled with prayers of the saints.

Their song exceeds any earthly masterpiece. They proclaim three supreme achievements of the Lamb (Revelation 5:9,10, paraphrased).

First, *He redeemed a ruined humanity.* "You have paid the death sentence for all of us!" Second, *He launched a world rescue.* "You purchased with your blood people out of every tribe, language, society, and culture!" Third, *He gained a global kingdom.* "Your people will rule the world with You!"

The singing expands to clouds of angels far out beyond the perimeter. It spreads to every creature in the universe (Revelation 5:13). Sight and sound exceed human comprehension. The Lamb of God sets His people free from all evil and launches the final stage of His global kingdom. He begins to rule the world population.

How Does Prayer Affect My Future?

A dilemma arises out of this cosmic inauguration. Something is not normal. Scripture says that redeemed saints are going to reign with Christ, but we will do this as priests (Revelation 5:10; 20:6). The problem is this: Priests are not rulers. Kings have that authority. Priests serve the temple in prayer, worship, praise, and song.

Yet here, in Christ's coming kingdom, priests will rule under Him! How can this apparent contradiction be reconciled? The answer unveils a priceless principle. As God's child, you will have dominion over part of His realm. You will do it as a priest.

People who receive Christ become eligible to pray. The apostle Peter calls us a *royal priesthood* (1 Peter 2:9). In the Old Testament, priests served as intercessors between man and God. The fact that we will rule as priests means that we will *rule by praying!*

What will be your job description when you reign with Christ? A second-level ruler carries three primary responsibilities. First, he assesses the needs of people in his domain. Second, he requisitions supplies for those needs. Third, he distributes those supplies to the needy areas.

What is your job description as a priestly intercessor today? It is exactly the same! Responsibilities you have on your knees are like those you will have on your throne. You assess human needs—burdens, cares, anxieties—that God entrusts to you. You requisition God's supplies for these needs by intercession. You allocate those supplies to needy places and people by faith. For example, you pray:

"Lord God, raise up laborers for the youth of that inner-city."

"Release provisions for that unemployed family."

"Heal that young mother with cancer."

"Impart saving faith to my lost friend."

"Raise up messengers to take Your good tidings throughout Saudi Arabia."

Your praying is training for reigning with Christ. That is why God created prayer. That is why He places such emphasis on prayer. Training in prayer is as important as getting answers. Now you can understand the Bible's significant emphasis on prayer. Challenges in prayer develop your maturity. They prepare you for rulership under the coming King of kings.

Although training for reigning is a significant role of prayer, receiving answers is also important. In our next chapter, we will discover why we can be assured of those answers. We will see the link between God's sovereignty and our prayers.

Prayer Response

My beloved King, I have missed important training through my prayerlessness. I ask for and receive Your gracious forgiveness. Help me to make up some of my lost training. I give myself to praying in training for reigning with You! In the name of Your Son, amen.

Personal Reflection

- To what degree are you building prayer into your present occupation?

- How might you use some current challenge for prayer training? Describe what you might do.

Practice Step

Practice some training for reigning with the King of kings.

1. Identify an area in which you are responsible.

2. Record this responsibility in a prayer notebook. Make it a focus of prayer for the next week. Pray about weaknesses, pleasures, or problems associated with your responsibility.

3. In your notebook, write Scriptures and insights that God brings to your mind during the week.

4. After one week, indicate any change you are experiencing in trusting God for your responsibility. Measure your progress on a 1–10 scale.

5. Plan your future development starting from the new high point that you have experienced this week in prayer.

6. Expand this praying to an additional responsibility entrusted to you, then another, and another.

CHAPTER 6

Our Prayers and God's SOVEREIGNTY

I s GOD IN CONTROL of everything? Any answer to this question creates a problem for prayer. If you answer "yes," you may ask: Why pray when God already knows what He is going to do? What difference can my prayers possibly make on the future? If you answer "no," you might wonder: Why pray if God is not in control of everything? How can I trust a limited God?

Which answer is right? How do my prayers relate to Almighty God?

Do My Prayers Change God's Will?

The prophet Isaiah took a hard look at the dilemma of God's sovereignty and praying people when he predicted the future of the Jewish people.

Jewish history reached a peak under King David and King Solomon. The people, however, had a problem. They repeatedly strayed from God to worshiping idols. As they did, their personal and national life became decadent and abhorrent to God. After all, these were God's people—the line from which the Messiah would come to save the world.

Isaiah lived under four kings (Isaiah 1:1). Two of them, Uzziah and

Hezekiah, were good rulers who faded in the end. The other two, Jotham and Ahaz, were wicked throughout their reigns. They brought destruction on the Jewish kingdom of Judah through national spiritual deterioration (2 Kings 5–20).

Isaiah saw national disaster coming. His report in chapter 59 of his book reads like a modern newspaper. A headline on his story might read: "Man Attempts to Block God's Will."

Isaiah calls out, "Attention, everyone! God is not paralyzed. He is not too weak for our problems. He is not deaf to our prayers. Our national emergencies are the natural fruit of our sins!" Isaiah lists these widespread offenses: murder, deception, filthy speech, injustice, corruption, crime, moral perversion, violence, conflict, unrighteousness, despair, guilt, rebellion, treachery, apostasy, oppression, corruption, and moral collapse.

Does this list of sins describe your country? How prevalent are they in your city and neighborhood? They signal coming judgment.

From verse 16, another headline might read, "God Appalled!" God was deeply disturbed by the moral state of the people in Judah —but not surprised. One situation, however, simply defies all reason. As evil propelled the population toward invasion and exile, almost no one asked God to step in and change the course! Almost no one prayed!

The attitude of the people was irrational. They knew that God loves His people, that He was longing, able, and waiting to rescue their nation. They also realized that God hates and punishes sin. Their prophets had all made that point clear. God's hearing is excellent; His power is absolute. No one can duck the consequences of immorality and idolatry. Still, the dying nation refused a moral ambulance and no intercessors came to rescue the dying patient!

How Can My Prayers Affect My Country?

God cannot endure the insanity described by the prophet Isaiah. God refuses to be victimized or to overlook the blatant disregard for His just rules. So He moved into action. First, He searched for an intercessor. Finding no one to plead for His people, He resorted to force to get their attention. His military tactic is described in Isaiah 59:17,18.

God put on a military uniform to execute national punishment —a breastplate, a helmet, and garments of war. He prepared to pour out fury, judgment, and wrath. The nation would pay for her sins because she refused to ask for forgiveness. The forces of Babylon start gathering for invasion. His people were going into captivity.

God's purposes will be fulfilled. He *will* have a people for His name. No person or thing can impede His plan. The final outcome of God's dealings with His wayward people is stated in verse 19:

> So shall they fear the name of the Lord from the west, and His glory from the rising of the sun; when the enemy comes in like a flood, the Spirit of the Lord will lift up a standard against him.

Our modern world is also in desperate need. We are hurtling toward God's judgment. As in ancient Judah, God looks for intercessors to bring the needs of our country before Him. Our prayers make way for the God of the universe to act on behalf of peoples, governments, and nations. If believers do not pray and bring God's power to bear, the result will be destruction. God is sovereign. His plans will be accomplished with or without us.

This is the point of the story for us: Prayer does not change God's will because He does not change (Malachi 3:6). But prayer affects the way in which He carries out His will!

What If I Do Not Pray?

As we have seen in the example of Judah, God reserves two options for action: A, if you pray; and B, if you do not.

Under option A, God extends mercy and grace through the work of intercessors. When you pray, you receive the benefits of His compassion and forgiveness. In love, He waits to be wanted. He waits to be asked.

Under option B, God moves by force, based on His sovereignty and holiness. His purposes must be accomplished. He will not abandon the world He loves.

Over the centuries, God has offered this choice. God made option A clear to Solomon:

> "If My people who are called by My name will humble themselves, and pray and seek My face, and turn from their wicked

ways, then I will hear from heaven, and will forgive their sin and heal their land" (2 Chronicles 7:14).

Four hundred years later, God made both choices clear to the prophet Ezekiel:

Option A: "I sought for a man among them who would make a wall, and stand in the gap before Me on behalf of the land, that I should not destroy it."

Option B: "But I found no one. Therefore I have poured out My indignation on them; I have consumed them with the fire of My wrath; and I have recompensed their deeds on their own heads," says the Lord God (Ezekiel 22:30,31).

The New Testament affirms God's alternatives.

Option A: "Ask, and it will be given to you; seek, and you will find; knock, and it will be opened to you" (Matthew 7:7).

Option B: "You do not have because you do not ask" (James 4:2).

The options we choose will have far-reaching effects. When we choose option A, we become part of God's infinite plan. If we choose option B, we miss the privilege of being used by God and the spiritual blessings that provides.

How Can My Prayers Fit Into God's Plan?

Is God, then, in control of everything? Yes, He certainly is. He would not be God otherwise. *The way He orchestrates control, however, is in the hands of praying people.* The choice for a nation is to pray or to perish. It is revival or wrath. It is intercession or judgment.

People who are spiritually lost cannot pray for their country. They must first call on the Lord for their own salvation (Romans 10:13). National courses of events are affected only by praying believers in Christ Jesus, as shown in 2 Chronicles 7:14. It is God's people who evoke God's nationwide blessings through their prayers. Christians carry a critical responsibility for their fellow citizens!

You and I alone cannot saturate our country with prayer. We can, however, saturate the part of our country that God has entrusted to us. Praying for our territory is His way to accomplish His plan. Paul urges us to action in 1 Timothy 2:1–4:

Therefore I exhort first of all that supplications, prayers, inter-cessions, and giving of thanks be made for all men, for kings and all who are in authority, that we may lead a quiet and peaceable life in all godliness and reverence. For this is good and accept-able in the sight of God our Savior, who desires all men to be saved and to come to the knowledge of the truth.

These verses show us how we fit into God's plan. Our praying is the starting point.

"Prayer laid the tracks," said Bishop Wellington Boone, "where the gospel was going to come."[1] Will you offer your prayer life to God as an action channel for His sovereignty? Part 4 will provide some exciting opportunities for prayer ministry. But those doors open only to believers who submit to His call. Christian, commit yourself to prayer today. It is our one way to change the future for our friends and family—and even our country!

We have glimpsed the action in God's arena. We proceed now to view key players integrating their roles to accomplish the purposes of our God. In Part 2, "Action in God's Arena of Prayer," we will see members of the Trinity making our prayers a galaxy of wonders and miracles. We will watch battles in God's arena. We will decide to take or to forfeit His victory!

Prayer Response

Holy God, I am staggered by the importance you place on the prayers of Your people. You plan to effect Your will through our prayers. I under-stand this truth in my mind. Now help me to digest it in my heart. I ask You to nurture prayer as a part of my life. In the name of Jesus, I sin-cerely pray. Amen.

Personal Reflection

- What are some changes in your praying that could affect the des-tiny of your family, community, or nation?

- What are some outcomes you desire for them?

- Do you believe they can be prayed into effect? Why?

Practical Step

After reflecting on the questions above, share your desires with some Christian friends. Discuss what they think about the questions. Using what you shared, pray for each other and that you will deepen you prayer desires.

PART TWO

Action in God's Arena of PRAYER

Real praying is a costly exercise but it pays far more than it costs. It is not easy work but it is most profitable of all work. We can accomplish more by time and strength put into prayer than we can by putting the same amount of time and strength into anything else.

R. A. Torrey, *The Power of Prayer*

CHAPTER 7

Prayer and God the FATHER

WHEN A YOUNG couple marry, one of the most important parts of their wedding ceremony is the exchange of rings. The groom slips a wedding band on the bride's finger and then she places a wedding band on the groom's finger. We all know what the ring symbolizes—a never-ending love and commitment to each other.

The circle is used in other ways as a symbol of completeness or an unbroken pathway. We have all heard the phrase "a circle of friends." To symbolize this, friends will form a circle and join hands. "Circle the wagons" comes from the American pioneers' practice of drawing their wagons into a circle whenever outside danger threatened them. The circle provided protection because no one's undefended side was exposed. The "circle of life" refers to nature's ability to replenish itself year after year without stopping.

A circle is also a wonderful picture of how prayer works. First Thessalonians 5:17 tells us to pray continually. Rather than picturing prayer as a single missile, such as an arrow, that wings its way to God, I like to consider our prayer life as a circle. Like the budding relationship of the newlyweds, prayer doesn't stop but is an ongoing action involving all the members of the Trinity and the pray-er. At the same time, each person involved in the prayer circle has a definite role to play.

So far we've taken an overview of God's theater of operations and

59

how prayer fits into the panorama of the universe. In this section, we'll take a closer look at the action within the circle of prayer and the roles each Person in the Trinity plays. We'll begin with God the Father to whom we offer our prayers. Then we will cover the three intercessors mentioned in our key verses, Romans 8:26,27. As you read, study the many verses provided and practice the prayer applications. See if you can become more deeply involved in the cosmic action taking place right now in God's arena of prayer!

The Source of Everything

Our Heavenly Father

High at the top of God's action arena, the Father occupies the chief position. Early Bible prayers such as the one found in Genesis 14:18–20 address Him as "God Most High." Isaiah describes Him as "He who sits above the circle of the earth, and its inhabitants are like grasshoppers, who stretches out the heavens like a curtain, and spreads them out like a tent to dwell in" (Isaiah 40:22). This is a picture of how God rules over His theater of operations.

Yet even with all His supernatural power, the God of the universe craves your praying. Can you imagine that? God Almighty has spanned space to redeem and listen to tiny human beings. He loves you and longs to interact with you. That is astounding!

How can you know this? God has performed numerous marvels to bring you to Himself. To generate your praying, He:

- Created the universe (Acts 14:15)
- Created your soul (Genesis 2:7)
- Inspired the Bible (2 Timothy 3:16,17)
- Sent His Son (John 3:16,17)
- Sacrificed His Son (1 Peter 3:18)
- Chose and called you (John 15:16)
- Continues to work through His Son (Hebrews 7:25)
- Planned our world's destiny (Revelation 5:8–10)

A staggering statement about the Father is given in Romans 11:36:

"Of Him and through Him and to Him are all things, to whom be glory forever. Amen." In other words, the verse announces, "God is the source, the means, and the goal of everything that exists!" The verse is speaking of the Father—*your* Father. His name is Almighty, and prayer begins with Him.

Though He eagerly awaits your prayers, He can receive you only on His terms. You must meet Him in all His perfection; He cannot change His nature. Do not fear, however. Jesus has satisfied all imperfections in your behalf. Come to your Father, confessing your disqualifications and trusting confidently in the perfect righteousness of your Savior, Jesus Christ.

How Does the Father Do His Work?

Biblical prayers are centered in the heavenly Father. He is restoring the earth to Himself. He is working through intercessors to turn people away from ungodliness (Romans 11:26,27).

He draws the world to Himself in three ways, each defined by a phrase found in Romans 11:36.

First, *the Father* **starts** *your praying* ("of Him...are all things"). Your prayers do not begin with you. They originate with your heavenly Father. Pray expectantly, therefore, knowing that He is the One who entrusted your requests to you.

Our Lord Jesus practiced this truth. While Christ was on earth, He pointed prayer to the Father when He taught His disciples to pray: "In this manner, therefore, pray: 'Our Father...'" (Matthew 6:9).

You may have wondered: *Why pray when God already knows everything?* The answer: Because love will not impose itself on the beloved. True love waits. God, in love, waits to be wanted. He waits for you to come to Him in prayer.

Second, *the Father* **equips** *your praying* ("through Him...are all things"). "Trying to pray" or "saying your prayers" is not the richest way to communicate with God. Regard Him, rather, as your Father. View Him as joyfully bringing you to Himself.

My wife, Mary Jean, experienced this fatherliness of God during the early stages of cancer some years ago. As she prayed, God revealed Himself to her as holding her in His arms in a rocking chair. Looking back, we calculate that her healing began about that time.

Scripture makes clear that effective prayer focuses on God the Father. There are four reasons for this focus:

1. God established prayer for His own glory (John 14:13).

2. Answers to prayer are assured by the Father's love (Romans 8:32).

3. Strength in our prayers comes from the power of His might (Ephesians 6:10,11).

Our approach to God must give Him the honor He is due. *Respect* for your heavenly Father is essential in prayer. Focus your prayers and trust on Him alone. Idols disgrace the Father (2 Corinthians 6:16–18). Even good things can become an idol. For instance, money is beneficial when received from the Father with thanksgiving, but becomes an idol when it displaces the Father in your heart. Idols confuse, obstruct, and deface your prayers. Get rid of them!

Third, *the Father receives your praying* ("to Him…are all things"). Our attitude toward prayer is the same as our attitude toward God, because prayer is communicating with Him. Our view of God determines the quality of our prayers.

- Prayer is lonely when we regard Him as distant.
- Prayer is annoying when we see Him as weak.
- Prayer is tasteless when we consider Him as stupid.
- But prayer is intriguing when we behold His majesty.

"We *ask* as a hungry beggar or a lost traveler," wrote Robert Foster, a veteran staff member with The Navigators ministry. "We *seek* as a gold miner, a petro-geologist, or Admiral Byrd at the South Pole. We *knock* as the Avon lady, the magazine salesman…If we love to give good gifts…how much more does God!"[1]

What Does My Father Want of Me?

A father in Montana accidentally killed his little son with a car. For many days after the funeral, the father kept repeating, "I wouldn't have done it for the world!" The tragedy had no purpose in his mind.

God's Son, Jesus, also died a tragic death. But when His Son died, our heavenly Father did not say what this earthly father said. Jesus was sent to earth to die. In fact, the Father ordered the events that caused the execution of His own Son! This selfless act made a way for you to come to Him—to talk to Him in prayer. He loves you, and He wants your communication that much!

Problems with prayer indicate problems in our relationship with God. The better you know Him, the more you can trust Him and the more you will desire His fellowship in prayer.

Do you remember the story of the prodigal son, found in Luke 15:11–32? The son broke fellowship with his father by taking his inheritance and leaving home. He wanted freedom to do as he pleased.

When he humbly, repentantly returned, his father welcomed him with joy and excitement. The son could not enjoy his father's generosity until he came back.

Like the wayward son, we honor the Father most by coming to Him just as we are. All God desires is a reverent, trusting, seeking attitude. He supplies all cleansing, covering, and connection necessary for wrongs that block His blessing. God is not bothered by outward appearance; He sees the attitude of our heart.

"Who may ascend into the hill of the Lord?" David asks in Psalm 24:3,4. He answers his own question: "He who has clean hands and a pure heart." God receives praying people who are cleansed, forgiven, sincere, and truthful.

Jaundiced attitudes produce a crippled prayer condition. Such emotions grow out of distorted views of the heavenly Father. Some people are angry with God, thinking that He has acted wrongly. Others seek escape from Him, considering Him to be unkind. Many others envy an acquaintance's prosperity, believing the Father is unfair.

Reactions of this kind slander God and damage our praying. Would parents likely consider requests from children who regard them in this way? The psalmist speaks God's verdict, "If I regard iniquity in my heart, the Lord will not hear" (Psalm 66:18).

If you discover a wrong attitude toward God in your praying, reach for God's remedy.

1. *Admit the dishonor this attitude places on Him.*

2. *Repent.* Return to the Father from your wicked ways. Seek Him. Revelation 2:5 exhorts everyone to "remember therefore from where you have fallen; repent and do the first works."

3. *Confess your sin to Him.* Confess (agree with God about) the grief you have brought to His heart (1 John 1:9).

4. *Accept the forgiveness of Calvary.* Christ has already made the way to fellowship with God (1 Peter 3:18).

5. *Receive the Spirit of Jesus in prayer*—the Spirit of love, humility, peace, and trust in the will of the Father (Galatians 5:22,23). Leave to Him the settling of wrongs you have suffered.

6. *Worship your heavenly Father.* Praise and adore Him for one attribute at a time. To help you, a chart of His attributes is given in Appendix B.

Now that we have a clearer understanding of the Father's central role in our praying, we can discover the roles of the three-mentioned intercessors in our key verses. We will turn to our human role first.

Spiritual warfare is being waged at this very moment. But because of our relationship to the Father, we have a vital role to play in the victory!

Prayer Response

Holy Father, I confess my wrongful attitude toward You. I have hurt You. I repent of it with sorrow. I marvel that You nailed this sin to the cross with Jesus, together with all my other sins. Because He paid my penalty for sin, I ask for and receive Your forgiveness. Cleanse my disposition. I give the wrongs of the past over to you. Fill my temperament with the same Holy Spirit that dwelled in Jesus. I receive these answers because I am asking in Jesus' name. Thank you, dear Father. Amen.

Personal Reflection

- Since prayers come from the Father, should you wait to pray until He stirs you to do so?

- In what ways might you know when God is stirring you to pray?

- Is it all right to pray to Jesus and to the Holy Spirit? What reasons do you have for your answer?

- Do you really believe that repentance and confession on our part are sufficient to obtain forgiveness for prayerlessness? Give a reason for your answer.

Practical Step

Study Appendix B, "The Attributes of God," to help you more deeply understand God's nature. Use the information to strengthen your trust in God for your praying.

After you complete the next three chapters, answer the Personal Reflection questions again to see if your responses have changed.

CHAPTER 8

My Role in God's ARENA

MARTIN LUTHER described the importance of praying: "To be a Christian without prayer is no more possible than to be alive without breathing."[1]

God, in His amazing grace, involves praying people in His world plan. Praying Christians are at a lowly six o'clock position in the arena of prayer—but we are there! We are the first-mentioned inter-

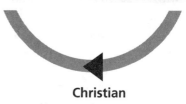

Christian

cessor in our key verses. The reason is thrilling: we are in the center of the battle!

I watched a nature film years ago that showed a fight between a mongoose and a cobra. A mongoose is a small animal about the size of a squirrel; a cobra is a deadly snake. In the film, the rodent stalks the coiled snake.

The cobra strikes several times, but the mongoose always darts back just beyond the snake's reach. Suddenly, faster than the eye can follow, the two become a writhing ball of skin and fur. The motion soon stops and the little mongoose drags a dead cobra home to eat.

Satan confronts us much like a cobra. Christians alone are no match for his evil powers. God, however, has given us access to His unlimited power. Like the tiny mongoose, we are conquerors! Prayer is our access to God and His power.

God came into your life when you received Jesus Christ as your Savior. He waited to be invited because He loves you. That invitation is the very first prayer God wants to hear from anyone. He comes to you as your personal Answerer!

How Far Do My Prayers Reach?

The prophet Daniel discovered a galaxy of wonder in prayer. He wrote a book in the Bible about it that carries his name. Daniel was exiled from Israel to Babylon along with thousands of his countrymen. They were still there when the Persian Empire conquered Babylon. Daniel learned from studying Scripture that Israel's seventy-year captivity would soon end (Daniel 9:2).

This godly man could have watched the countdown as a spectator. Instead, he began three weeks of fasting and prayer for the future. His tenth chapter tells the story. Daniel prayed desperately for a week. Nothing happened. A second oppressing week passed with no relief. After a third week, his anguish lifted.

In verses 4–7, we read that Daniel and some friends went for a breath of fresh air. Walking by the Tigris River, a brilliant personage met them and knocked Daniel to the ground. His companions ran for cover.

The person may have been an angel because he reported heavenly action. Or this visitor may have been the eternal Christ. His description is much like the glorified Christ whom John met in Revelation 1. In either case, this person was a superhuman messenger. He handled high-ranking spiritual forces somewhere between earth and heaven. He now reassured and strengthened Daniel with his hand. Daniel would need that energy.

The messenger described for Daniel what had been happening in the heavens over the past three weeks. Action started, he said, the day Daniel began to pray (verses 12,13). The prayer was instantly registered in heaven and an answer was issued.

Immediately, however, a "prince of Persia" intervened to block the answer. That prince, the demonic force ruling the Persian Empire, is identified in three ways. He had access to a battleground in the heavens; he was totally opposed to God's plans; and he exercised supreme influence in the realm.

Alerted and alarmed by Daniel's prayer, this spirit-emperor arose to block God's answer. The battle grew into the largest star-war ever described. The kings of Persia's 127 provinces rose and entered the conflict. The messenger says, "I had been left alone there with the *kings* of Persia" (Daniel 10:13). They fought for 21 days—the exact time span of Daniel's fasting and praying!

These were not human kings. This was not an earthly battlefield. Daniel's answer was being delivered from heaven. This was a hierarchy of ruling spirits who motivated and energized nations within the empire.

Michael, an archangel and commander of angelic armies, was alerted to the super-war. He flew to the aid of the embattled messenger, most likely with his angelic legions as in Revelation 12:7. The messenger broke through the battle lines to meet with Daniel, leaving the battle under Michael's command. The messenger had come personally to deliver an answer to this persistent intercessor.

The content of that answer explained the immensity of that battle. The message is recorded in chapters 11 and 12 of his book. Small wonder that demonic powers united to stop God's response to his praying. The message revealed God's plan to the end of time, including:

- Persian, Greek, and Roman empires; kingdoms of Egypt and Syria (Daniel 11:2–35)

- The coming evil world dictator (Daniel 11:36–45; 2 Thessalonians 2)

- The great world tribulation and Christ's forcible repossession of the earth (Daniel 12:1–7; Revelation 15–20)

- Survival of Daniel's people, the Jews (Daniel 12:1)

- The resurrection of the dead and eternal life (Daniel 12:2,3)

- Preparation of the saints for God's kingdom (Daniel 12:10)

- Reward of the inheritance for the faithful (Daniel 12:12,13)

Like Daniel, we too reach into the realm of heaven with our prayers. Few conflicts are as great as his, but as you see through his example, our prayers produce changes beyond our range of sight. God's forces battle to make our prayers effective. Further, today we are living after the events of Calvary, after Christ has disabled and disarmed world demonic powers. We therefore have greater advantages than Daniel had!

How Do People Fight Cosmic Battles?
At the time he fasted and prayed, Daniel had absolutely no clue about the war in the skies. All he knew was that he had a burden that compelled him to pray. His prayer yields special guidelines for us today.

Principle 1: *Present your burden to the Lord until He lifts it.* Daniel learned an astonishing fact. His praying had caused all the action! The messenger told Daniel, "From the first day…, your words were heard; and I have come because of your words" (Daniel 10:12). Had Daniel stopped praying, the action would have ended.

Principle 2: *Use your prayers as a channel for God's action.* Daniel's praying and the heavenly war were simultaneous operations.

Principle 3: *Hold onto God's power in connection with evil strongholds until the Father overcomes the enemy.* That's the persistent role of intercessors as presented in Philippians 4:6,7: "Be anxious for nothing, but in everything by prayer and supplication, with thanksgiving, let your requests be made known to God; and the peace of God, which surpasses all understanding, will guard your hearts and minds through Christ Jesus."

Do I Need to Fight in Prayer?
Do modern times call for Daniels? Does God plan to use your prayers for spiritual wars on national or city levels?

Yes, He does! Conditions Daniel saw then are also bad today. Violence is accelerating. Evil is increasing more and more. At the same time, unprecedented doors are opening to the gospel.[2]

Christ hit Satan's strategy at Calvary. An expanding search is under way for intercessors like Daniel who will keep hitting Satan with that same resurrection power. God's people are taking a heavy barrage from the enemy. On the other hand, huge new prayer initiatives worldwide are blasting evil strongholds. The call is out for more intercessors to complete the Great Commission of Christ!

Two Personal Prayer Plan guides are provided in Appendix C. The first worksheet is a one-week guide; the second covers up to four weeks. (The first one is followed by a sample that you can use to fill out your own worksheet.) Based on Acts 1:8, they can expand the range of your daily prayer outreach and help you organize prayer issues that God entrusts to you. The Practical Step at the end of this chapter will show you how to apply them to your prayer life.

The circle of prayer is not yet complete. You will find more in-depth information about how prayer works as we go on to the second and third intercessors mentioned in our key verses. I encourage you to apply your discoveries to your Prayer Plan as we go along.

Prayer Response
Thank You for the pioneering prayers of Daniel. Help me to follow his example. I am amazed at the cosmic range You have given to prayer. I want to make prayer my primary work in life. Strengthen me to sustain prayer for Your burdens, like Daniel did, until You lift them. Teach me persistence to follow the words of 1 Peter 5:7 and cast all my cares upon You. In Jesus' name. Amen.

Personal Reflection
- Would God have carried out His plan without Daniel's prayer?
- How effective do you think your praying is?
- Does God do *any* work without prayer? Explain your thoughts.

Practical Step
1. Start with the One-Week Prayer Plan. Read Acts 1:8, then spend some time filling out your Personal Prayer Plan. Use it for four weeks. Revise it, adapt it, and make it a life pattern for your praying. God has a big prayer menu for you. Your Prayer Plan will help you manage most of your prayer responsibilities.
2. As you use your daily Prayer Plan, God will expand your prayer ministry. To spread your prayer targets over more days, fill out and begin using your One-Month Prayer Plan.

CHAPTER 9

My Coach, the
HOLY SPIRIT

D O YOU EVER GET that wistful feeling," asks Robert Foster, "that there are other things more effective, even more desirable, than prayer? This explains why far too many of us are busy in attempting great things for God, rather than expecting great things from God in a humble attitude of prayer."[1]

Self-reliance injures a prayer life. Success often puts prayer in a hospital (Deuteronomy 6:10–13). Trouble, on the other hand, can really motivate a person to pray. Psalm 107 reports four troubles that trigger prayer: emergencies, bondage, death, and financial crisis. When people with these problems call on the Lord, He rescues them. If only they would pray and praise Him on shore, yearns David, they could handle storms.

The Day of Pentecost in the Book of Acts was as important to the early Church as Christmas is to us. On the Day of Pentecost, the Holy Spirit moved His residence to earth.

God the Holy Spirit is limitless and He is everywhere all the time. Before Pentecost, however, His seat of administration appears to have been in heaven. His residence within men was temporary. (See Exodus 31:3; Judges 6:34; 14:6; and 1 Samuel 16:13,14 for examples.) The Day of Pentecost brought about a tremendous difference. Jesus had announced earlier, "I will pray the Father, and He will give you another Helper, that He may abide with you forever, even the Spirit of truth" (John 14:16,17). The change in residence is described by Paul, "Do you not know that your body is the temple of the Holy Spirit who is in you?" (1 Corinthians 6:19).

One reason the Holy Spirit came was to help people to pray. We see His promise to intervene in our key verse, Romans 8:26, "Likewise the Spirit also helps in our weaknesses. For we do not know what we should pray for as we ought."

The Second-Mentioned Intercessor

The Holy Spirit operates at a three o'clock position in the prayer arena, and He is the second-mentioned intercessor. He occupies that position because He plays a vital role between the Father and the praying believer. Here are some things the Bible teaches about the work of the Holy Spirit in prayer:

Holy Spirit

- He is the Spirit of grace and supplication (Zechariah 12:10).

- He came upon Jesus like a dove when He was baptized and praying (Luke 3:21,22).

- The Spirit came to earth in answer to the prayers of Jesus (John 14:16–18).

- One hundred twenty disciples, praying in unison for ten days, received the arriving Holy Spirit (Acts 1:15; 2:1–4).

- First-century Christians, praying in the Spirit, evangelized the world.

In 1999, Americans watched thrilling field action as the U.S. Women's Soccer Team met the Chinese team to determine the 1999 Women's World Cup championship. News commentators spoke admiringly about the incredible skills and ability of both teams. U.S. defensive work, spearheaded by Michelle Akers, was a major factor in preventing the Chinese from scoring and in winning the game.

A key person for the U.S. team was coach Tony DiCicco. He watched the action on the field and assessed the kind of plays that would work best. He decided who would substitute for players on the field and when. His view was objective. Without his efforts, the players would not know how to best use their skills to win the game.

The Holy Spirit is the world's head coach in prayer. As God, He has a perfect view of the "field" of the universe. He knows all the perfect "plays." Jesus introduced Him as a paraclete—one called alongside to help us. He is a priceless team leader.

The Spirit's arrival on earth was more valuable, Jesus said, than for Jesus Himself to continue living here. The Spirit of God has come to live within us and improve our praying! He "helps our weaknesses" in at least eight ways.

How the Spirit Mends Our Prayer

He Works To:	*His Therapy:*	*Scripture References:*
Assure Us	Revelation	1 Corinthians 2:9,10
Draw Us	Invitation	Revelation 22:17
Enable Us	Preparation	John 16:13,14
Guide Us	Intercession	Jude 20, 21
Inspire Us	Consolation	Acts 9:31
Instruct Us	Communication	Romans 8:26
Qualify Us	Sanctification	1 Peter 1:2
Sustain Us	Expectancy	Romans 8:23

It is reassuring to know that we need not be perfect in our prayers. God even provides a Helper who helps us pray! He prays *for* us, *through* us, and *in* us. At first glance, these three prepositional phrases seem similar, but they are distinct actions which the Holy Spirit takes in our behalf. Let's look at these three actions.

The Spirit Is Praying *For* You

Do you sometimes feel overloaded with prayer needs? "Don't ask me to pray for another thing," said one lady. "I have too many things to pray for now!" She had not asked the Holy Spirit for a God-sized prayer capacity.

The Holy Spirit Himself intercedes for us. He prays for your capacity, direction, development, and success in prayer. Ask Him to help you organize your praying. The Personal Prayer Plan worksheets in

Appendix C will give you the format for a plan. Use them as an aid to praying as the Holy Spirit leads. Spread your prayer load over a week, or even a month if necessary. Do not try to pray for everything every day.

Pray for issues the Spirit places on your heart—whether they are on your prayer list or not. He gives limitless variety in the Father's will that goes along with His overall plan for your prayer direction. One day, for example, you may be burdened to pray about an unexpected need for money. On the next day, your prayer concern may be for the salvation of a loved one. You may not have intended to spend time on those items, but your prayers are drawn to them like a magnet.

What is happening? God the Holy Spirit is designing your daily prayer menu. He is expressing His groanings through you, praying through you. This is a major component in "praying in the Spirit" (Ephesians 6:18).

The Spirit also prays for your prayer moods! "We do not know what we should pray for as we ought" (Romans 8:26). Technically, this phrase does not say "what we should pray *for*," it says "what we should pray." This verse speaks of more than the content of your prayers. It includes your feelings.

Moods can flatten prayers like ripe grain in a storm. You may not feel like praying at times, so you pass it by. And a huge store of supplies in heaven's warehouse remains unharvested (James 4:2).

The Spirit gives drowsy Christians a new passion in prayer. "Is there anything too hard for Me?" God asked of a discouraged Jeremiah as Jerusalem was going up in flames (Jeremiah 32:27). He asks the same question today of despondent Christians living in a wicked city. He asks it of a neighbor near a high school or college campus. And of the small church trying to minister in a rural community.

Paul writes of the insights we can receive through our communion with God:

> It is written: "Eye has not seen, nor ear heard, nor have entered into the heart of man the things which God has prepared for those who love Him." But God has revealed them to us through His Spirit. For the Spirit searches all things, yes, the deep things of God (1 Corinthians 2:9,10).

The Spirit will lift you above discouragement and arouse you to call on the Father. He will reveal outpouring wonders of God. But He waits until you ask.

The Spirit Is Praying *Through* You

Our key verse reminds us that "the Spirit Himself makes intercession for us with groanings which cannot be uttered. Now He who searches the hearts knows what the mind of the Spirit is" (Romans 8:26).

"Groanings" of the Holy Spirit means anguished yearnings beyond words. Twice the apostle Paul uses the same word earlier in the chapter. The first in verses 19–22 refers to creation: "For the earnest expectation of the creation eagerly waits for the revealing of the sons of God…We know that the whole creation *groans* and labors with birth pangs together until now."

Agonies of the animal food chain, natural catastrophes, and human cruelty illustrate groanings throughout creation. Two phrases in this passage are highly significant: "revealing of the sons of God" and "birth pangs." Groaning in creation anticipates the reign of Christ on earth.

The second groaning is in verse 23: "Even we ourselves [believers] *groan* within ourselves, eagerly waiting for the adoption, the redemption of our body." Christians yearn for physical deliverance as well as their spiritual rescue. We long for Christ's return. Sickness, pain, and disappointments cause us all to "eagerly wait for…the redemption of our body." We pray with longing the prayer Jesus taught His disciples: "Your kingdom come. Your will be done on earth as it is in heaven" (Matthew 6:10).

Groanings, then, are longings for the fulfillment of the Father's world plan. The Holy Spirit prompts this kind of praying in God's people. He intercedes with the same type of longings (groanings) that permeate all creation. He yearns for completion of God's plan for the world.

Groanings of the Holy Spirit come to you as concerns or burdens. Parents sob for wayward children. Pastors weep over worldly congregations. Praying citizens agonize over evil nations. You experience these intense desires because the Holy Spirit in you feels that way about them. You rest these cares in God's hands (Philippians 4:6,7).

Here is an amazing conclusion: *It is your prayers that give expression to the otherwise unexpressed groanings of the Spirit!* The Holy Spirit seeks to pray God's eternal purposes into effect through you. Anglican commentator H. Alford explains the role of the Spirit and prayer in Romans 8:

> The Holy Spirit is here spoken of as dwelling in us; in this indwelling He makes the intercession. This view...accepts the prominent thought of the previous part of the chapter (verses 9, 11, 14, 16), and implies not only that by this indwelling, we are taught to pray what would otherwise be unutterable (Calvin, Beza), but that the Holy Ghost himself pleads in our prayers.[2]

The highest kind of praying, therefore, is the praying of the Holy Spirit through you. The Bible calls it "praying in the Spirit" (Ephesians 6:18; Jude 20).

God is waiting on your praying! Practice the words of an old spiritual: "Ev'ry time I feel the Spirit movin' in my heart, I will pray." Obey the Spirit in prayer and bring your guilt, pressures, and schedules to Him. Admit problems you have in praying. Ask His aid and turn to Jesus in confession and faith where you need it. Use your prayers to release the sighing and longings of the Spirit.

The Spirit Is Praying *in* You

The Son of God descended to earth at Bethlehem, entered a human body, and redeemed the human race. At Pentecost in Jerusalem, the Holy Spirit moved His seat of administration from heaven to earth. He formed, entered, and filled the Church as Christ's body and vehicle of action on earth.

To this day, the Spirit is completing God's global plan through the marvel of prayer. Children of God are the temple of the Holy Spirit. His temple is designed for prayer (Mark 11:17).

The picture is a priest offering up prayers in the beauty and holiness of God's dwelling place. The Holy Spirit is praying *in you* as God's temple—whether you pray alone or with others. It is the Holy Spirit who is filling, motivating, energizing, guiding, and joining your prayers with His own. His praying makes prayer priceless.

The most significant part of your prayers, therefore, is the praying of the Holy Spirit in you. The Spirit is using your praying to express His own groanings. When you pray under His direction, He does His marvelous praying *in your prayers*.

How Can I Pray in the Spirit?

The Bible speaks twice about praying in the Holy Spirit. The first, in Ephesians 6:18, is closely related to spiritual warfare. "Praying always with all *prayer and supplication in the Spirit*, being watchful to this end with all perseverance and supplication for all the saints."

The second, in Jude 20 and 21, deals with spiritual growth and endurance. "But you, beloved, building yourselves up on your most holy faith, *praying in the Holy Spirit*, keep yourselves in the love of God, looking for the mercy of our Lord Jesus Christ unto eternal life."

Praying in the Holy Spirit essentially means allowing Him to pray in and through you. His praying in you involves seven factors:

- *Being filled with the Holy Spirit.* Being filled with the Holy Spirit means allowing Him to direct and control all of you. Ephesians 5:18,19 directs you to be filled with the Spirit so you can pray and worship in the Spirit. One naturally leads to the other. If you are unfamiliar with this marvelous provision of the Holy Spirit, read *Have You Made the Wonderful Discovery of the Spirit-Filled Life?* (published by Campus Crusade for Christ). This tract has brought untold numbers of Christians into His promised fullness and power.

- *Trusting in the grace of God.* Zechariah 12:10 speaks of God's "Spirit of grace and supplication." You do not induce His praying. You release it by praying for the burdens He lays on your heart.

- *Praying Scriptures back to God.* In 2 Peter 1:21, we read that the Scriptures are inspired by the Spirit. Focusing on God's Word is integral to praying in the Spirit. (In Chapter 11, we will learn how to pray using Scripture.)

- *Walking in the Spirit.* Galatians 5:16 exhorts us to walk in the Spirit to conquer the flesh. Dr. Bill Bright uses the term "Spiritual Breathing" to describe how we walk in the Spirit. Practice

Spiritual Breathing by breathing out the bad air of unconfessed sin as you meet with God in up-to-date confession. Once you've confessed your sins, breathe in the good air of a fresh infilling of the Spirit. Then move forward in your Spirit-filled life and your prayers.

- *Growing in the fruit of the Spirit* as described in Galatians 5:22,23. Associate yourself with a Christ-centered fellowship of Christians who stimulate spiritual maturity in each other (Ephesians 4:11–16).

- *Getting the mind of the Spirit.* This is addressed in Romans 8:27. Surrender your will to God continually like Jesus did in Gethsemane, so you can pray according to His will as evidenced in 1 John 5:14,15.

- *Listening to His guidance* as the Antioch Christians did in Acts 13:2,3. Pray both for the *goals* the Spirit lays on your heart and for the *ways* He wants you to pray. His plans and procedures are as important as His purposes. An ounce of obedience is worth a pound of prayer (Acts 5:32).

Praying in the Holy Spirit provides the benefits of His own intercession. He brings satisfaction and fulfillment to our daily prayers. It is relaxing—not laborious—to receive and relay the longings of the Spirit in prayer.

For some intercessors, praying in the Spirit involves using a prayer language. This practice frees their spirit from the limitations of language and gives greater flexibility in communion. For others, praying loudly or silently are very important for "praying in the Spirit." For still others, including me, praying in the Spirit involves praying with the mind rather than with the tongue. This kind of thought-praying provides a release from the limits of speech and allows both spirit and mind to soar in communion with God.

Users of one practice urgently need to respect the others, so that we don't grieve the gentle Holy Spirit. Ephesians 4:3 urges us to try "to keep the unity of the Spirit in the bond of peace." Appendix D offers valuable guidelines by noted Christian historian C. Peter Wagner for united prayer meetings. I encourage you to read this material to help you in your praying with others.

To put into practice the essentials discussed in this chapter, use the following steps:

1. *Once you are sure you are filled with the Spirit, pray the things He lays on your heart. Give the Spirit the time He desires to pray through your prayers.* Do not quit too soon. Keep at it until you can cast all your cares upon Jesus and He replaces your anxieties with His peace.

2. *Seek to improve in your praying.* First, remember that poor prayers are better than no prayers. Any prayer becomes an instrument in the hands of God. Then do not quench the Spirit by neglect nor grieve Him by misbehavior that can hinder your praying (1 Thessalonians 5:19; Ephesians 4:30). Missing prayer for a day interrupts His mighty work.

3. *Practice Spiritual Breathing.* When you grieve the Spirit by sinning, immediately practice Spiritual Breathing to cleanse yourself and restore your fellowship with God.

4. *Grow in expressing the Spirit's longings in prayer.* Make these actions a lifelong adventure: maintain a prayer list, allow expandable time, pray your way through the Scriptures, follow the burdens of your heart, and obey the promptings of the Spirit.

Prayer Is Active Battle

Does it seem absurd to review prayer requests in a prayer group, then repeat them in prayer before the Lord? It's not absurd. Prayer lists themselves are not prayers. Requests become prayers only when they are *expressed* to God, in either words or thoughts. An unexpressed desire is only a wish. Prayer is active battle in God's theater of operations.

The Rev. John Robinson was pastor to the Pilgrims who first journeyed to America. As his people embarked for the New World, he gave perceptive insight on praying in the Spirit:

> God first works true prayer in humble hearts by "pouring on them the Spirit of grace and supplication" (Zechariah 12:10). The Holy Spirit then reveals what is to be prayed for, and leads in the manner of prayer. All true prayer is by "the teaching of the Spirit of God."[3]

God does not need information from your prayers. He knows everything on any list before the list is even compiled. A prayer list is not for His benefit, but for *yours*, to remind and guide you in prayer.

God wants you to communicate your anxieties to Him. In this way, you *articulate* the mighty praying of the Holy Spirit.

Now that we have seen the role of the first and second intercessors, we can turn our attention to the third. His role completes the cosmic circuit of prayer.

Prayer Response

Beloved Spirit of God, I give You my praying to be a channel for Your intercession. Increase my awareness of Your groanings and grant to me Your guidance to express them well. Teach me to regard Your prayer interests as more important than mine, to blend my prayers with Yours. I ask this in the name of Jesus. Amen.

Personal Reflection

- If you are walking in the Spirit, can you be sure that all your impressions will come from Him?

- How can you "test the spirits" to find out if your ideas are truly coming from God? (See 1 John 4:1.)

- Have you experienced a "prompting" of the Holy Spirit in prayer? How would you describe this experience?

- How might you improve your ability to recognize the leading of the Spirit?

Practical Step

Pause now to seek the mind of the Spirit for something He wants to pray into effect through you. If you are alone, write out a care that is on your heart and pray for it. Keep it before the Lord, as He leads, until you can cast that care upon Him. Then thank Him for His answer and watch to see how He will fulfill it.

If you are in a group, seek the mind of the Spirit by identifying a common concern. Join in prayer for that concern, believing that the Spirit has entrusted it to your group. Notice the difference it makes for your group to pray in the Spirit.

CHAPTER 10

Jesus, My Connection IN HEAVEN

A S WE LEARNED IN Chapter 3, a third intercessor steps forward in Romans 8:27: "He who searches the hearts knows what the mind of the Spirit is, because He makes intercession for the saints according to the will of God." This, of course, is the Son of God. Placed in the nine o'clock position in God's prayer arena, He is un-named to focus attention on His action. Five proofs assure us that Jesus is that divine intercessor.

Jesus Christ

Jesus is a member of the Trinity. Verse 26 tells us that this intercessor searches the hearts of pray-ing Christians. Only God can do that. Jesus, God the Son, is qualified to be this intercessor.

This Person is not the Holy Spirit because He knows the mind of the Spirit. The pronoun "He" cannot refer to the Spirit in this context.

He is other than the Father because He makes intercession according to the Father's will. Using textual unity, we consider that both of the "He" pronouns refer to the same Person.

The searching of hearts is a function of God alone. Many Scriptures make this clear, including Jeremiah 17:10: "I, the Lord, search the heart, I test the mind, even to give every man according to his ways, according to the fruit of his doings." One member of the Trinity, however, is singled out as having this authority (Revelation 2:18,23).

Jesus is specifically named as an intercessor in this same chapter of Romans. Chapter 8, verse 34 says: "It is Christ who died, and furthermore is also risen, who is even at the right hand of God, who also makes intercession for us."

Jesus Is Your Prayer Power

Evangelist Merv Rosell tells of a bully who often beat up on a smaller boy after school. One day the small boy came home with a black eye. His older brother asked him what had happened. The small boy explained the problem.

"Tomorrow," said the big brother, "I want you to walk slowly past the place where this bully attacks you."

"Slow!" exclaimed the little boy. "When I run he almost kills me. It will be worse if I walk slow!"

"Don't worry," said his brother. "I have a plan. Trust me."

The next day, the small boy fearfully walked slowly into the danger zone. As the bully started toward him, the big brother leaped from hiding and thrashed the bully soundly. No attacks occurred again.

Hebrews 2:11 says that Jesus is our Big Brother. He works with His people in a similar way. He crushed Satan at Calvary and delivers all who trust in Him.

Yet when Jesus was on earth, He was a disappointment to the nation of Israel. They looked for a Messiah with political power. The Messiah who came, however, exercised a greater power—*prayer power*. In doing so, He dashed the hopes of those who cheered at His triumphal entry to Jerusalem. Instead, He chased the merchants out of God's temple, declaring: "Is it not written, 'My house shall be called a house of prayer for all nations'? But you have made it a 'den of thieves'" (Mark 11:17).

His earthly ministry did not end His work as our Big Brother. Train your spiritual telescope on Jesus in heaven today. Total authority in the universe is in His hands (Matthew 28:18–20). His power is absolutely supreme. What is He doing with it? He is using His power in unending prayer!

Hebrews 7:25 says of Jesus: "He is also able to save to the uttermost those who come to God through Him, since He always lives to make intercession for them." This verse reveals Jesus' powerful labor in heaven. He is joining your prayers to His own in several ways. Jesus Christ is:

- *Praying with ultimate power.* "All authority has been given to Me in heaven and on earth" (Matthew 28:18).

- *Transferring your requests to God.* "He who searches the hearts... makes intercession" (Romans 8:27).

- *Sustaining praying people.* He intercedes for those who are coming to God (1 Peter 3:18).

- *Protecting you.* He is actively working in our behalf with His intercession (Romans 8:34).

- *Pleading your cause in heaven.* He is our Advocate with the Father when we sin (1 John 2:1).

Jesus Is Your Prayer Guarantee

Hebrews 7:25 also tells us that "He is also able to save to the uttermost." His saving includes everything *from* which we are saved (God's displeasure) and also everything *for* which we are saved (God's purposes). There is no handicap in your prayers through Him!

Jesus' enormous work in heaven has a two-way flow. In the book *Holiest of All*, Andrew Murray writes of this high-velocity pathway as portrayed in the Book of Hebrews. Jesus Christ "has passed through the heavens" (Hebrews 4:14) to serve as "Minister of the sanctuary" (Hebrews 8:2).[1] This means that Christ is representing you before the Father as your great High Priest. He is your celestial attorney, pleading your cases at the center of ultimate power. And He is doing a perfect job of it.

According to Hebrews 8:6, He is also Mediator of the covenant representing the Father to you. He is working with equal perfection in both directions—you to the Father and the Father to you. Jesus sees that your prayers get answered (John 14:13). He is also delivering all of the Father's gracious gifts toward His people (Ephesians 1:3).

Painful situations make it hard to believe that Christ's work in heaven is perfect. "How could this happen?" His followers cry. "Something up there must have gone wrong! God must be angry with me."

While God is teaching you to pray like Jesus, your petitions sometimes clash with the Father's will. Prayer disappointment can result from a wrong attitude, such as, "Not *Your* will, but *mine* be done." Jesus prayed in the opposite way, and the Father answered by raising Him from the dead (Hebrews 5:7).

Christ is interceding for the will of the Father in behalf of praying people. He is doing it twenty-four hours a day—through delights, delays, or denials. Happy are intercessors who demonstrate, by waiting for the Lord, that His will is good and acceptable and perfect (Psalm 40:1–3; Romans 12:2).

Jesus Is Your Prayer Partner

A literal translation of Hebrews 7:25 is "He is able to save...the coming-to-God-by-Him ones." As we discussed earlier, "coming to God" is a synonym for prayer. (Appendix E lists forty-six other expressions for prayer.) Christ is praying for praying people, whether they are coming to God initially for their salvation, or repeatedly in intercession. Calling on the Lord to be saved is the beginning of an eternal life of prayer. "You received the Spirit of adoption by whom we cry out, 'Abba, Father'" (Romans 8:15).

But coming to God goes far beyond that initial cry for salvation. Have you ever awakened at night in a desperate, pounding panic? You toss, turn, and fight the pillow in frantic anxiety. How you wish there was something you could do at that hour of the night. There is!

Our key verses in Romans 8 open up a spiritual sunrise: *When you pray, you place intercessory material into the prayers of the Lord Jesus Christ.* Your praying is loading up His mighty praying hands. Take your panic as critical groaning from the Holy Spirit. Leap into prayer. Labor then and there to transfer your emergencies over to the intercession of Jesus. Give Him the opportunity to release the Father's provision in heaven—right there in the night hours.

Jesus Is Your Prayer Attorney

Trust the praying of Jesus more than the prayers of people. *The praying of Jesus is the power of your praying!* The strength of your prayers does not come from the number, skill, or saintliness of human beings. It comes from the all-powerful praying of Jesus.

Today Jesus Christ is your heavenly attorney, coming before the judicial bench of God in your behalf. As your attorney, He performs numerous supernatural actions in heaven. When you pray in His name, He:

- *Receives your prayers.* "Come to Me, all you who labor and are heavy laden, and I will give you rest" (Matthew 11:28).

- *Interprets your prayers.* "He makes intercession for the saints according to the will of God" (Romans 8:27).

- *Expands your prayers.* "[God the Father] put all things under His feet, and gave Him to be head over all things to the church, which is His body, the fullness of Him who fills all in all" (Ephesians 1:22,23).

- *Presents your prayers to the Father.* "There is one God and one Mediator between God and men, the Man Christ Jesus" (1 Timothy 2:5).

- *Sustains your prayers (never stops).* "He always lives to make intercession for them" (Hebrews 7:25).

- *Implements your prayers (sees that they get done).* "Whatever you ask in My name, that I will do, that the Father may be glorified in the Son" (John 14:13).

Jesus Christ is the ultimate intercessor. He is the praying Christ of the wilderness, the early mornings, the mountains, the Upper Room, and Gethsemane. Today this same Jesus is inheriting the nations through His praying (Psalm 2:7,8). Whatever the need for an advocate, Jesus performs it for God's people.

Isn't it amazing that this same Jesus, the only One who has the perfect right to approach the Father, also lives in the heart of every true Christian? Paul describes Jesus as abiding in His children:

> To them God has chosen to make known among the Gentiles the glorious riches of this mystery, which is Christ *in you*, the hope of glory (Colossians 1:27).

Recall now the cosmic drama revealed by the intercession of Jesus. When He arose from the dead, He regained the total global power that people had given to Satan (Matthew 28:18). Forty days later, He ascended back to heaven (Luke 24:50,51). Even since that ascension day, He has devoted His supreme authority to prayer.

Our key verses tell us that Jesus is praying for the groanings of God the Holy Spirit. He finds these groanings in the praying of His inadequate, believing, interceding children. He is presenting those groanings to God the Father and getting the prayers accomplished on our planet!

Further, the intercession of Jesus is so excellent that the results exceed superabundantly everything we are able to pray for or imagine (Ephesians 3:20)!

This is the marvelous work of our Lord Jesus that goes on in heaven when we pray. Without Christ's role in prayer, our pleadings to God would surely go no higher than the ceiling. He is the Agent who searches our hearts and brings our requests to God. The praying of Jesus is the power we engage by praying in His name!

Treasures in Delayed Prayers?

One thing doesn't seem to fit the marvel of Jesus' praying. Even when all conditions are right, we sometimes do not receive the answers we requested. What is wrong? The Bible shines a brilliant light on this question. God delays or denies answers at times to teach lessons that could not be learned in any other way. "Everyone who asks receives," said Jesus in Matthew 7:8. Your answers may not be what you expected, but you do get an answer!

Sometimes delayed answers provide blessings more valuable than immediate answers. Jesus illustrated this truth on a journey outside His homeland. In Matthew 15 a woman from Tyre and Sidon (modern Lebanon) encountered Jesus during His only foreign trip. This is the only event recorded on that journey.

The woman cried out to Him to help her demonized daughter. Jesus' slowness in acting taught her vital principles about waiting:

The Principle of Attention. The woman's first concern was her daughter. Jesus' silence shifted her attention from her daughter to Him. The disciples noted this fact when they reported to Jesus, "She cries out *after us*" (Matthew 15:23).

Most prayers begin with a need. As the answer is delayed, your attention turns upward. You begin to see your need against the background of almighty God. The lesson is crucial for everyone. Faith can only be as strong as its object. Waiting on the Lord fastened the mother's attention on Jesus and thus transformed her faith. It can do the same for you.

The Principle of Character. Jesus taught the woman that her goal had a lot to do with her answer. In verse 24, He says, "I was not sent except to the lost sheep of the house of Israel." To paraphrase, "You don't have the right racial credentials to ask me anything."

She accepted the lesson. Her response was to worship Him by saying, "Lord, help me!" She grasped the idea that Christ is Lord and that He is seeking worshipful people. He gives freely to people with the character to seek Him alone.

Delays in answers are often designed to sift our praying and build our character as well as to gratify a need. Praying people of every race and background need to take aim on Jesus—His will, His way, and His glory.

The Principle of Attitude. The woman learned that humility is priceless to God. When Jesus said, "It is not good to take the children's bread and throw it to the little dogs," He was not being unkind. He was using a common cultural slur to refine her attitude. He loves people and was making a point. Note her response in verse 27: "True, Lord, yet even the little dogs eat the crumbs which fall from their masters' table." She was saying, "I am not a Jew, so I make no claim on You. I am totally unworthy. I come only on the basis of Your mercy. I have seen Your power and I trust in Your goodness."

That is what Jesus waited to hear. Humility is the basis on which Christ meets anyone. If answers were on the basis of merit, no one would be qualified to receive them. We all need His mercy.

The woman received her answer and her daughter was healed that very hour. But more than that, she received instruction for a lifetime.

Do not resent delayed answers. They are openings for priceless lessons from your Lord. They can only be learned by waiting on Him.

This completes the circuit of God's work in the world. The panorama places your prayers in the arena of God!

Since the three Persons of the Trinity are united in answering our prayers, we know with assurance that our requests are of supreme importance to God. Our prayers are more than one-time events. They are part of a lifestyle of walking with God.

As any soldier knows, hit-or-miss strategy will not win a war. Believers who pray now and then will not accomplish much either. God has a greater plan for our praying. In Part 3, "Living in God's Prayer Arena," we will explore the transformation experienced by those who continually meet God face to face.

Prayer Response
Lord Jesus, thank You for showing me how Your praying relates to mine. You have made me a connector between Your intercession and that of the Holy Spirit. I am amazed at that! Joyfully I begin afresh to bring You the longings the Spirit entrusts to me. I worship You for this privilege and calling. Teach me the lessons I need to learn. Thank You! Amen.

Personal Reflection
- Why do you think the supreme power of Jesus is needed in your praying?
- List some ways in which you can better utilize the praying of Jesus.
- How have you observed the power of God released through prayer?

Practical Step
Write in your journal or share with a prayer partner a long-delayed answer to prayer. Add indicators of partial answers. Confess any element of unbelief that has disrupted your persistence in prayer. Identify spiritual lessons you have learned through the delay. Renew prayer with thanksgiving for the supreme power of Jesus' name.

Use Appendix E, "Synonyms for Prayer," as a study to help you search the depths of our prayer access to God.

PART THREE

Living in God's Prayer ARENA

Prayer is God's life-giving breath. God's purposes
move along the pathway made by prayer to their
glorious designs. God's purposes are always mov-
ing to their high and beneficial ends, but the
movement is along the way marked by unceasing
prayer. The breath of prayer is from God.

E. M. Bounds, *The Complete Works*
of E. M. Bounds on Prayer

CHAPTER 11

Meeting God
FACE TO FACE

I MAGINE WITH ME the life of a newly wed couple who is committed to Christ. In the evening, they both come home from work and have a meal. Afterward, they may enjoy watching some television or going shopping together. Since they are conscientious about building a strong marriage, they try to communicate with each other, spend a few moments in devotions together before they go to bed, pray together at other times of the day, and work at treating each other with respect.

The years pass and they reach their tenth anniversary. They take a mini-vacation together to celebrate their love for each other. One evening over an elegant dinner, they reminisce about the highlights of their years together—the day he proposed marriage by hiding her engagement ring in a box of candy; the times they spent with good friends at a cabin beside the lake; the afternoon they were involved in a serious car accident but walked away without serious injury. Each memory is as precious to them as a pearl on the exquisite necklace he gave her for their tenth anniversary.

Yet it wasn't those events that made their relationship strong. It was the day-to-day effort of building closeness, of regarding each other's feelings and needs, of spending time together. The highlights were just markers along the road of their enriching marital growth.

This same principle is true for the arena of prayer. We often regard big answers to prayer as the most important part of our prayer life. We remember the illness that God healed, the time He brought financial relief during a crisis, or how He provided wisdom during a stressful situation with our children. Certainly, God's prayer blessings are priceless to us. Yet it is not primarily events in prayer that bring us closer to Him. It is day-to-day living in the arena of prayer. It is the intimacy we build with God and victories He gives (sometimes inch-by-inch) that develop our faith.

We can and should record prayer miracles and answers as markers in our growing fellowship with God. But in this section of the book, we will examine the value of living daily in God's arena of prayer.

The Radiant Life

The late evangelist R. A. Torrey lived close to God. I have in an old file an article in which he describes his experience living a radiant life. His words reflect the joy we can experience through our communication with God.

> I presume everybody has known someone whose life was just radiant. Joy beamed out of their eyes; joy bubbled over at their lips; joy seemed to fairly run from their fingertips. You could not come in contact with them without having a new light come into your own life. They were great electric batteries charged with joy.
>
> If you look into the lives of such radiantly happy persons ...not those people who are sometimes on the mountaintop and sometimes in the valley, but people who are always radiantly happy...you will find that every one is a man or woman who spends a great deal of time in prayer alone with God. God is the source of all joy, and if we come into contact with Him, His infinite joy surges into our lives.
>
> Would you not like to be a radiant Christian? You may be. Spend much time in prayer. You cannot be a radiant Christian in any other way. Why is it that prayer in the name of Christ makes one radiantly happy? It is because prayer makes God real.
>
> The gladdest thing upon earth is to have a real God! Oh, the joy of having a real God! I would rather give up anything I have in the world, or anything I ever may have, than to give up faith

in God. You cannot have vital faith in God if you give all your time to the world and to secular affairs, to reading the newspapers and to reading literature, no matter how good it is. Unless you take time for fellowship with God, you cannot have a real God. If you do take time for prayer you will have a real, living God, and if you have a living God, you will have a radiant life!

Do Torrey's words reflect the cry of your heart? Any Christian can experience a radiant life in the arena of prayer. The beginning point is sensing the presence of God.

How Can I Sense the Presence of God?

An old Methodist preacher gave some fascinating advice one Sunday night in my college days. "When you pray," he said, "don't start by saying things. First, pause until you can sense the presence of God."

What an idea! Who doesn't want to meet the living God? I decided to try it. My alma mater, Azusa Pacific University (then Pacific Bible College), required thirty minutes of devotional time each morning. It was an ideal time to try the preacher's idea. That period became a spiritual laboratory for me.

Kneeling by my bunk the next morning, I paused to sense God's presence. I paused, paused some more, and kept pausing. I found *no* sense of God's presence. What I sensed instead was a whirlwind of distractions—schedules, assignments, exams, and bills. Mind wandering ruled supreme!

It was the longest half hour I had ever spent. I endured the experiment because of student rules. We were not to work on class assignments, visit, or wander the halls. We were to be alone with God. I kept squinting at the clock to see how much time was left.

Then at 7:25 something changed. I remember the time from watching the clock. My brain slowed, and my attention came into focus on the Father. I could not see Him, but I looked into His face with my mind's eye. I exclaimed in silent wonder, "Lord, You're right here, and You are looking straight at me!" He had been there all the time, of course, but now I became aware of Him.

The last five minutes were wonderful, like catching a salmon or taking a first airplane ride. It was a thrill that was worth the twenty-five-minute struggle. It was fascinating to be with God, and I eagerly looked forward to trying it again.

The next morning was much the same, but it took only twenty-three minutes to sense God's presence. Once again, I knew from glancing at the clock. Wednesday required twenty minutes, Thursday nineteen, and so on down to a few seconds.

In time I came alive to three big principles. These truths have actually been anchoring saints in prayer from the beginning. They were new discoveries to me.

Principle 1: We need spiritual conditioning to pray, just as we need physical conditioning for athletic competition.
Can you imagine a world-class athlete skipping his training because he got up too late or because he wasn't in the mood? One common trait among successful athletes is self-discipline in training. Physical conditioning keeps athletes strong through the rigors of the game.

Spiritual conditioning is equally as vital in our Christian life. Like the time an athlete devotes to his sport, your spiritual conditioning involves the time you spend seeking God's face.

Scriptures are filled with God's call to seek Him. Second Chronicles 7:14 says, "If My people who are called by My name will humble themselves, and pray and *seek My face*, and turn from their wicked ways, then I will hear from heaven, and will forgive their sin and heal their land." Hebrews 11: 6 records, "[God] is a rewarder of those who diligently seek Him." Genuine prayer is built on intimacy with the Lord. God wants to meet us face to face. St. Augustine declared that our hearts are restless until we settle down and focus on God. Yet, strangely, that kind of intimacy seems unfamiliar to many of God's children.[1]

Practice the exercise of spiritual conditioning by seeking the Lord like Jacob did at Peniel. He wrestled with God and cried out, "I will not let You go unless You bless me!" (Genesis 32:26). Persevere in seeking God's face until you sense His presence. Set aside the time necessary to focus attention on your heavenly Father. You can do it. He's waiting for you.

Principle 2: Make your prayer distractions your prayer agendas.
Those college bills, deadlines, and duties of my spiritual laboratory were real needs. I later learned that they were part of God's prayer

agenda for me. Listing and praying over those "diversions" helped me focus on the God who knew about those needs and made it much easier for me to meet Him face to face.

Moses became a mighty man of God not so much for his heroic achievements as by his habit of bringing his concerns to God in prayer. We know this from the epitaph the Lord wrote for him. To this day, no one knows where the Lord buried Moses, but the epitaph is recorded in Deuteronomy 34:10, "Since then there has not arisen in Israel a prophet like Moses, whom the Lord knew face to face." Moses was great because he turned his problems into prayer agendas.

Is it possible to ask for anything you desire and also pray according to God's will? Listen to the words of Jesus: "If you abide in Me, and My words abide in you, you will ask what you desire, and it shall be done for you" (John 15:7).

Two conditions in this verse answer the questions above. You can pray for anything you want if: 1) you are abiding in Christ, and 2) His words are abiding in you.

"Abiding" means living together, like a family. Christ is receiving you in His love. Are you receiving and retaining His Word? To the degree in which you abide in Jesus, you can expect that your desires have come to you from the Holy Spirit. Asking for your desires under these conditions in praying according to His will! In this wonderful way, you can ask for and receive anything you desire because your desires will be His desires, too.

Principle 3: Pray Scriptures back to God.
I first learned to pray Bible portions back to God from a Chinese believer. He spoke about prayer as reading the Word of God. From him, I learned to listen in prayer as well as to speak. I adapted his ideas to my own needs and found them a marvelous aid in meeting God on a one-to-one basis. It is not difficult. Here is how you can do it:

- *Read a phrase or passage in the Scriptures, then turn it into a prayer.* Apply the passage to your life and talk to God about it.

- *Address the Lord in a way that is comfortable to you.* Use respectful phrases such as "Dear God" or "Heavenly Father."

- *Apply the A-C-T-S prayer method to that portion of Scripture:* Adore and worship Him, Confess sin, Thank Him for a blessing or answer to prayer, or Supplicate (ask) Him to supply a need.

- *Move on to the next phrase in your Bible and do the same.* Pray your way through a paragraph. Over time, pray through a chapter, then through a book of the Bible. At this writing, I am praying through the Bible for the fourth time. Each time through takes me about five years.

- *Write down insights that come to you.* Record your discoveries in a journal. In this way, you can build your own personal Bible commentary. Your personal journal will refresh you like an ever-flowing river refreshes a dry land.

Praying Scripture back to God adds the richness of a costly, fragrant perfume to prayer. This way of praying can help shape your thoughts, desires, and words. It is a communication that pleases the Lord and fulfills your soul!

The Benefits of Praying Scripture

Praying the Bible provides many benefits for a growing intimacy with God.

- *Your praying becomes two-way conversation.* As you pray, you listen to God's words as well as talk to Him.

- *Your mind focuses quickly on His truth.* As soon as you address Him, you find yourself face-to-face with Him. You are on common ground with the Lord!

- *Scriptures dredge up an ocean of content to pray about.* God's Word provides power, wisdom, and direction for our prayers. Hebrews 4:12 lays the foundation: "The word of God is living and powerful, and sharper than any two-edged sword, piercing even to the division of soul and spirit, and of joints and marrow, and is a discerner of the thoughts and intents of the heart."

- *Your mood improves.* God carries you along. All of us have times when we do not feel like praying. Praying Scripture helps build motivation; psalms are excellent for this.

- *You explore the Bible from God's perspective.* The view you will find is fascinating and will add expressions of surprise (such as "Wow!") to your spiritual vocabulary.

- *You explore God.* Jesus said, "You search the Scriptures...These are they which testify of Me" (John 5:39).

- *You digest spiritual truth.* In praying Scripture, the Holy Spirit applies the Bible to our life. We move from looking at the food to actually eating it! Jeremiah found inspiration by devouring the Word of God. "Your words were found, and I ate them, and Your word was to me the joy and rejoicing of my heart; for I am called by Your name, O Lord God of hosts" (Jeremiah 15:16).

- *You inspire our own soul.* By praying Scripture you will soar to new heights in God. A common practice in daily prayers is to read the Bible then pray. Merging the two multiplies the value of each.

- *You release the action of God.* His answers are prepared and waiting to be received through prayer. "It is written: 'Eye has not seen, nor ear heard, nor have entered into the heart of man the things which God *has prepared* for those who love Him. But God *has revealed* them to us through His Spirit. For the Spirit searches all things, yes, the deep things of God" (1 Corinthians 2:9,10).

- *You mature in your soul.* The more we become like Jesus, the more we understand God and become ever more intimate with Him. There is no shortcut to maturity. It is a reciprocating spiral. Time and practice in prayer are foundational to growth.

Eye-to-eye communication with God is more than a novelty or luxury. It is a personal visitation with a dear, celestial Friend. The essence of prayer is to meet God face to face by seeking His face, praying about your distractions, and praying Scripture back to Him.

These are not commands. They are highway markers to the bursting heart of God. This is the God who desires our fellowship and love. He has promised to give us all we need through His Son: "It is the God who commanded light to shine out of darkness who has shone in our hearts to give the light of the knowledge of the glory of God *in the face of Jesus Christ*" (2 Corinthians 4:6).

At this point, you may be thinking, *I have tried to seek God's face, but it just hasn't worked. I don't know what's wrong.*

One problem may be the condition of your heart. As people with a tendency toward sin, we are not always open to hear God when He speaks to us. How can we break our tendency to sin? In our next chapter, we will learn how to prepare our hearts for prayer.

Prayer Response

Loving Lord, how I often long to meet with you face to face. How can I arrange that kind of time? My schedule seems so full. Give me wisdom to make an adequate schedule. Yes, I do manage to find time for things I feel are important. And more and more, You are becoming most important to me. So help me exchange trivia in my schedule for quality time with You. I ask this in Jesus' name. Amen.

Personal Reflection

- Time is an important factor in prayer. We all have the same number of minutes and hours in our days. What are some specific ways in which you may arrange more time for prayer?

- At this point in your spiritual journey, how much daily time in prayer would you consider adequate?

- How much time do you think you will need later on?

Practical Step

Alone or in a group, pray your way through two or three verses of Psalm 23. Write down discoveries you receive from the Lord in the exercise.

CHAPTER 12

A Heart That God
WILL HEAR

G OD DOES NOT listen to everyone. One big reason is that sin
blocks prayer.

Orville Clutterham, a Christian friend of mine, is a Los Angeles police officer. He often chuckled about Christian drivers who "witnessed" to him to avoid a traffic fine.

He pulled over the driver of a college van one morning for a flagrant violation. Stopped by Orville's flashing red light, the driver leaped from his van with an open Bible. "Officer!" he exclaimed. "Have you heard about John 3:16?"

Orville kept on writing the citation. "Yes," he replied, "I know John 3:16. But my favorite verse is Psalm 66:18."

Surprised, the driver turned to the reference and read, "If I regard iniquity in my heart, the Lord will not hear." The driver humbly accepted the citation and paid the fine.

One of the basic principles of Scripture is that sin interferes with prayer. In his first letter, Peter tells us, "The eyes of the Lord are on the righteous, and his ears are open to their prayers; but the face of the Lord is against those who do evil" (1 Peter 3:12). How clean must one be to talk with God?

The question is crucial because God is absolutely holy. Angels chant, "Holy, holy, holy is the Lord of hosts" (Isaiah 6:3). They do not sing, "Power, power, power" or any of God's other attributes in triplicate. They choose to do so only of His holiness.[1]

Can I ever be holy enough to converse with God? Two laws are at work in the soul of a Christian. One is the law of God, which underlies prayer. The other is the law of sin, which disqualifies prayer. In Romans 7:22,23, Paul describes the conflict between these two laws: "I delight in the law of God according to the inward man. But I see another law in my members, warring against the law of my mind, and bringing me into captivity to the law of sin which is in my members."

Romans 8 has good news about the prayer-killing sins we battle. "The Spirit of life in Christ Jesus" (verse 2) is providing three major remedies for our uncleanness. These New Testament remedies provide holiness to unholy people and enable us to talk with God. The process of becoming holy is called *sanctification*. For each remedy, let us consider a question to help us understand our unholiness in relation to God's holiness, the source of all holiness.

How Much Has God Forgiven Me?

Without forgiveness, we could no more pray than we can land a rocket on the sun. *Positional sanctification* is God's remedy for the guilt we all have accumulated from the past. It is an exchange of our sins for the righteousness of Christ Jesus. That wonderful provision makes it possible for us to enter the blazing presence of a holy God. Here's how positional sanctification works.

At the cross, God the Father accounted all of your sins to Jesus and all of Jesus' righteousness to you. "The one with no experiential knowledge of sin, He made to be sin in behalf of us, that in Him, we might become God's righteousness" (2 Corinthians 5:21, my translation from the Greek).

When you were born again by faith, the Holy Spirit united you with Jesus and all He accomplished. The term "baptism" is used to describe how completely you were personally submerged into the Lord Jesus Christ. (Baptism means immersion in the Greek New Testament language.) Our new position in Christ is described by Paul in Romans 6:3,4:

> Do you not know that as many of us as were baptized into Christ Jesus were baptized into His death? Therefore we were buried with Him through baptism into death, that just as Christ

was raised from the dead by the glory of the Father, even so we also should walk in newness of life.

Without compromising His holiness, God the Father forgives all sinners who put their trust in Jesus. We are sanctified by the sacrifice of Christ Jesus in our behalf. We are *united* with the Righteous One. Through Jesus, the Lamb of God, we can boldly come to the Father in prayer. Our sinful record is wiped completely clean by His blood shed for us!

For this reason, Paul could say that worldly Christians living in the city of Corinth were sanctified (1 Corinthians 1:2). He called them saints even though they were not acting very saintly.

The blood of Jesus Christ puts us on praying ground (Romans 5:1,2). Christ's righteousness in you is complete! You have at this moment perfect access to the Father through the righteousness of your Savior.

This truth transforms a prayer life. Do not draw back in self-condemnation or in self-improvement. Pray freely in the righteousness of Christ. This is your position in Him, your heritage.

Can Christ Cleanse My Character?

Well, you may be thinking, *I am surely grateful to God my Father for declaring me righteous in Christ. But I still do not pray the way I should. It is often hard for me to want to pray, take time to pray, sense God's presence, or receive answers by faith. I do not have a good prayer life.*

To grow to your full potential in prayer, your righteous position in Christ needs to be applied to your ego—your inner self. God does this work when you fully surrender to Christ's control and receive the Holy Spirit's filling. The Holy Spirit is the Spirit of prayer —the Spirit of grace and supplication (Zechariah 12:10).

Notice two things about this surrender. First, *it must be full.* No partial surrender can make enough room for the Spirit's fullness. Second, *it must be final.* The Spirit will not honor an experimental or temporary surrender.

God's Spirit in you is stronger than the law of sin and death (Romans 8:2). But in love, God waits for your permission to act through the surrender of your will (Romans 12:1,2).

I remember the time when I made a full surrender to Christ. It involved yielding my ego to Him and all that was dear to me. My surrender included persons, possessions, the future—everything. I became a living sacrifice. I accepted a death sentence on my self-centered life, which Paul calls "the flesh." I did it because I finally wanted Jesus more than myself.

Do you know what I discovered? The funeral notice became more like a wedding. It is not hard to say to your future mate at your wedding, "All possessions I share with you." You love this beautiful person. This is how Jesus appeared to me when I looked and saw Him there!

I stepped off the throne of my life and gave it to Him. It was then easy to pray, "Holy Spirit, will you now fill all the areas of my life that I have dominated?" At that moment, I received the communion of the Holy Spirit like a fresh, gentle wind. Christ replaced my self-centeredness with His presence. A love for prayer started to increase. I exchanged my independence for His rulership and my lusts for His love. I shared my whole being with Him. I opened all my heart to be His home.

I call entry into Spirit-filled living *pivotal sanctification* because here God's child enthrones Jesus as Lord in his or her heart. That is the crux, the turning point toward Spirit-filled living. Paul urges pivotal sanctification for everyone:

> This is the will of God, your sanctification: that you should abstain from sexual immorality...For God did not call us to uncleanness, but in holiness. Therefore he who rejects this does not reject man, but God, who has also given us His Holy Spirit (1 Thessalonians 4:3,7,8).

My father and his brother, my Uncle Loren, were horse trainers in their early years. I learned from Dad that there are two ways to "break" a horse so it will let you ride. One is to get on the horse and let it kick and buck until it yields to your control. That's the cowboy procedure that draws crowds to rodeos and movies. It pictures the way I used to pray.

The other way is to tie a rope around the horse's two front legs. When resistance begins, a small tug on the rope brings the horse to its knees. In that position, the animal quickly becomes a better learner. God began to use this gentle way with me.

While I am on my knees in prayer, I am a better learner. Formerly, the Spirit helped me to pray. Now He was released to pray His prayers through me. That's what the Bible calls "praying in the Spirit":

> But you, beloved, building yourselves up on your most holy faith, *praying in the Holy Spirit,* keep yourselves in the love of God, looking for the mercy of our Lord Jesus Christ unto eternal life (Jude 20,21).

As I matured in my faith, "praying in the Spirit" became a way of life for me. Then it was not difficult to grow in biblical, loving, trusting prayer.

Is this a step that you need to take? Fear it no more than escape from a cage. Jesus gave His all for you "for the joy that was set before Him" (Hebrews 12:2). Your full surrender to Him will have the same effect on you.

How Can I Clear Hindering Relationships?

Another kind of prayer-hindering sin is wrong behavior. Despite our good intentions, we stumble.

A third kind of cleansing is necessary, therefore, to mature in prayer. This cleansing is called *progressive sanctification.* We must apply God's holiness to our conduct. This is also called "walking in the Spirit." In Galatians 5:16, Paul urges us to pursue this lifestyle. "Walk in the Spirit, and you shall not fulfill the lust of the flesh." John invites us to live a life pleasing to God:

> Whatever we ask we receive from Him, because we keep His commandments and do those things that are pleasing in His sight. And this is His commandment: that we should believe on the name of His Son Jesus Christ and love one another (1 John 3:22,23).

Later in that same book, John gives a pointed quiz about bad relationships. "If someone says, 'I love God,' and hates his brother, he is a liar; for he who does not love his brother whom he has seen, how can he love God whom he has not seen? And this commandment we have from Him: that he who loves God must love his brother also" (1 John 4:20,21).

John raises a serious prayer problem. Is there anyone with whom you have a strained or broken relationship? Have you taken the initiative to restore that relationship? Do you love that person as Jesus commanded? If not, you are blocking answers to your prayers!

Troubled relationships grieve the Spirit, neutralize the gospel, and tie prayers in knots. Bill Gothard, founder and director of Basic Youth Conflicts, offers some very helpful steps to restore damaged relationships. From my own experiences, I wish to adapt his points for people struggling with prayer-hindering relationships.

- *Examine your own heart.* What attitude or conduct on your part may have contributed to this loss of fellowship? Have you offended or mistreated that person? Or do they perceive that you have? Do they have a grievance against you? (See Matthew 5:23, 24.) Or have you reacted to someone in an un-Christlike way? Have you rejected that person in your heart? Have you spoken against him or her? Do you love that person in Christ?

- *Confess to God your part of the wrong as sin.* Turn from that sin. Put it away from you. Repent of it. Receive God's forgiveness provided in the cross of Christ, and rejoice in the fresh forgiveness of Jesus.

- *Has the other person wronged you? Forgive that person unconditionally, just as God in Christ has forgiven you* (Ephesians 4:31,32). Jesus paid for this individual's penalty on Calvary. Do not require anything more from him or her than the cross of Christ. Release your hostility to Jesus.

- *Love this person by faith.* Loving someone who offended you may be humanly impossible. You can do it, however, by faith in Christ who lives in you. He commands us: "A new commandment I give to you, that you love one another; as I have loved you, that you also love one another. By this all will know that you are My disciples, if you have love for one another" (John 13:34,35).

  Take the time you need to love by faith. Wrestle out the struggle before the Lord. Tell Him in your own words, "Father I do not love this person. But because it is Your command, I ask You to provide the love I do not have. By faith in Your supply, I now take that step. I here and now choose to love this person."

This is the "good fight of faith" (1 Timothy 6:12). I can tell you from personal experience that it works. If you are a Spirit-filled Christian, love from God will be released, flowing from God Himself.

- *Go to your estranged friend and confess the wrongful part you played in the breakdown.* Make right any area in which you have wronged the other person. This is called restitution. Ask him or her to forgive *you.* Try not to leave until the other person says, "I forgive you." When he or she does so, the matter will be resolved. One word of caution: When you go to the other party, do not accuse him or her, even though this person's wrong may be worse than yours. Your initiative may bring this individual to repentance, but this is not your main goal. You need to clear your conscience before God.

    You may not be able to resolve every issue. Our responsibility is to carry out *our* part toward reconciliation. "If it is possible, *as much as depends on you,* live peaceably with all men" (Romans 12:18). If you do not resolve the issue, you will at least restore your prayer power.

I have conducted many weddings during fifty years of ministry. Two couples stand out as examples of clearing bad relationships. Both couples were new Christians and did not know each other.

Prior to her spiritual conversion and marriage, each wife had participated in an immoral relationship. Now the women were haunted by guilt. Each wife felt like her former non-Christian partner was saying: "We'll do it again. If you refuse, I'll make it all public!" Deeply troubled, each wife came with her husband to me for post-marital counsel.

I asked each wife, "Was there some degree of cooperation on your part in that past relationship?"

"Well, yes," was the response of both women.

"Have you received the Lord's forgiveness?"

"Yes."

"Do you know where this man works?"

"Yes."

Remembering Bill Gothard's counsel, I outlined a plan for them. "I suggest that you and your husband together go to this man's place of employment and speak to him privately. Acknowledge your past sin with him. Give testimony of your relationship with Christ and the forgiveness you have received from Him. The presence of your husband will validate your testimony. Confess your part in the past wrong, and *ask him to forgive you!* Try not to leave until he says, 'I forgive you.'"

Both couples agreed to do this. Within two weeks, each couple returned with a report of praise. When meeting with the couples, the men involved in the past relationships were at first embarrassed and attempted to minimize the past. Upon insistence, however, each man agreed to forgive the woman.

No restoration occurred or was expected in either case, but both couples were set free from agonizing bondage. The conscience of each bride was cleared. Freedom, peace, and joy in the Lord were restored.

A clear conscience is crucial in prayer. The procedure in the above story is also effective for restoring other Christian relationships. If the step is painful, remember that disqualified prayers and an ongoing sense of guilt will be far more painful.

The Importance of Sanctification

God's forgiveness and cleansing are available through sanctification. Our relationships with others also depend on sanctification. God's graciousness means that we can be forgiven, which frees us to live holy lives through His power.

Positional sanctification separates us from our sinful record. We receive this position the moment we receive Christ. God declares us holy because we are united to the absolutely Holy One. Jesus opens the way for our prayers.

Pivotal sanctification happens when, by an act of our will, we surrender ourselves to God's will as a lifelong commitment. The Holy Spirit transfers the control of our lives from self to Jesus. He opens the way for us to become more godly. Our prayers are released from bondage to our ego into the wonderful will of God.

Progressive sanctification results in conduct that increasingly reflects God's holy nature. This is carried out in the vital area of our relationships with others.

Therefore, the cleansing of sanctification in all three forms underlies our effectiveness in prayer.

So far in Part 3, we have explored the importance of meeting God face to face and learned that God hears the prayers of the righteous. Now we can discover the pathway to helping our faith grow in the arena of prayer. That pathway leads us to the Ladder of Faith.

Prayer Response

My forgiving Father, I bring to You my strained relationship with [name]. I confess to You my wrongs in the situation [anger, rejection, revenge, bitterness]. I do not love this person and do not really want to forgive him. I have wicked pride in my heart; I know it, and I need your cleansing. I ask You to change me. Any price is worth the freedom to pray.

Lord Jesus, I surrender my ego to You—my whole being—as a living sacrifice. I receive Your filling, Holy Spirit, and ask You to take control of all the areas that I have controlled and kept back from You. Thank You for forgiving me completely, purifying my heart, and filling me now with Your love.

And now I forgive [name], just as You have forgiven me. I believe that You love [name] just as much as You love me. By Your grace, I now take the step by faith to love [name] with Your love in me.

Strengthen me now to confess my wrongs to this person. Grant [name] grace to forgive me. Thank You for removing the enmity from my heart, and restoring my fellowship with You in prayer. I ask this in the name of Jesus. Amen.

Personal Reflection

- Have you at times sensed a special burden to pray for a person or a need? Describe these burdens.

- Do you believe that those burdens were actually groanings of the Holy Spirit? Why?

- How might you learn to be more sensitive and responsive to the promptings of the Holy Spirit?

Practical Step

Share with one or two trusted friends a difficult relationship in which you are involved. Listen to your friends' concern, too. Talk over any of the above steps you will need to take to resolve problems in your difficult relationships. Pray for each other and commit to support one another. To avoid delays or detours, schedule times to hold yourselves accountable to each other.

CHAPTER 13

Growing in FAITH

DAWSON TROTMAN founded the Navigators to encourage Christian disciples to teach spiritual principles to others. His work started with a hillside prayer group overlooking San Pedro harbor in California. He and a handful of men prayed for Navy ships lying at anchor. In time, God gave them a ministry on every one of those ships. Later they prayed for countries to which those ships sailed. Today The Navigators ministry has spread to those countries, representing all continents of the world.[1]

The prayers of those men led to faith in an enormous God. His answers exceeded all they could ask or imagine. *In the same way, people just like you move mountains by faith!* Faith-generating prayer produces world changes, "for whatever is born of God overcomes the world. And this is the victory that has overcome the world—our faith" (1 John 5:4).

Five levels of faith are revealed in Scripture. They form a five-step spiritual ladder I call the Ladder of Faith. Each step we will cover includes a corresponding Bible reference and an action point. The Ladder of Faith diagram demonstrates a procedure to help our faith grow. This growth doesn't happen all at once, but it is a process, like all other growth in our lives.

The growth of our faith is determined by our view of God and our response to His nature. Each step we take brings us into deeper intimacy with Him.

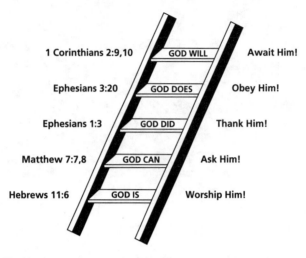

The first four steps on the faith ladder are our responsibility. Therefore, when your faith is weak, check the ladder's lower steps for any actions you need to take.

Step 5 is God's responsibility. Our part involves listening for His instructions and developing a willingness to await His timing, His wisdom, and His way.

Step 1:   *God Is*   Worship Him!   Hebrews 11:6

Hebrews 11:6 states, "Without faith it is impossible to please Him, for he who comes to God must *believe that He is,* and that He is a rewarder of those who diligently seek Him."

Your faith began when you received Jesus Christ as your personal Savior. In that moment, you came to know God in personal reality. You met the true and living God. You recognized Him to be big enough, wise enough, and close enough to answer your prayers.

Faith expands through worship. Worship is exploring and admiring God. The better you know Him, the more you can trust Him!

Faith is more than merely knowing something to be true. It is *entrusting* yourself to a person or object in which you have confidence. You trust anything to the degree to which you understand its nature. You trust your neighbor to watch your home because he has proved himself faithful in other things. You trust your teenage daughter with your car because she has proved that she is a competent, safe driver.

How much do you trust God? If we lack faith in our all-powerful, all-wise, all-loving God, we are actually doing something ridiculous. We are like the woman who was asked about her first airplane flight. "It went all right," she said, "but I didn't let my full weight down on the airplane during the whole trip."

She did not understand how nonsensical her actions were. She kept her feet off the floor because she thought that the aircraft would be lighter. In fact, she had relied more on the aircraft than she realized.

Our God upholds the universe! Yet in our weak faith, we are like that woman on the airplane. No matter where we go or what we do, we are always "held up" by our God. We trust His laws of nature. We receive His daily blessings such as sunshine and rain. Our faith now needs to transcend these truths and encompass all of life. We can "put our weight down" onto God's promises because He is always faithful.

To develop a strong faith in your Lord, make worshiping Him a central part of your life. Invest blocks of time in exploring Him in His Word. Admire Him and adore Him. Worship Him for His attributes. (See Appendix B.) Survey His greatness, His nature, His love. Your faith will parallel your growing acquaintance with Him.

Step 2:   *God Can*   Ask Him!   Matthew 7:7,8

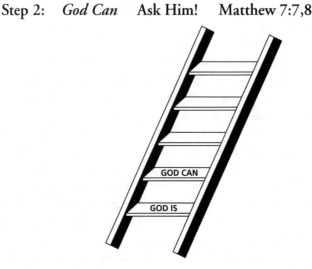

The more we realize that God is alive and real, the more we can believe that God is capable of doing great things. Paul demonstrated this progression in faith. "I know *whom* I have believed," he writes, "and am persuaded that He is able to keep what I have committed to Him until that Day" (2 Timothy 1:12).

Paul, in this same chapter, traces his growth in faith through prayer and worship. In verse 1, the great apostle worships Christ for his own life and calling. Out of that worship Paul goes on to communicate grace, mercy, and peace to Timothy (verse 2). As Paul grew in his acquaintance with God, he was able to commission Timothy into public ministry for Christ. He did so by the Spirit of power, love, and a sound mind (verse 7). Paul could trust Christ in personal suffering and imprisonment, and for the future (verse 12).

I suppose that every Christian ministry can give testimony to faith that grows out of worship. We start with the vision for a big need and a big God. Results come from the fact that worshipful, obedient prayers connect the need and our big God.

This kind of connection became real to me at Manila '90, a Campus Crusade evangelism conference in the Philippines. I was to lead a training seminar for national prayer coordinators as part of that massive event. Despite extensive preparations, our team arrived to find that all arrangements had fallen apart. Lodging for participants had been canceled. People with scholarships couldn't come. Materials for printing had not been received.

I called our Filipino staff together for desperate prayer and worship. The next note in my diary is dated two weeks later. "Today we graduated national prayer coordinators for 34 countries! Our *God who is able* had accomplished the humanly impossible.

Asking is also a part of believing. Asking and receiving occur at the same time. Both are present tense verbs in the Greek, showing continuous action. Literally, Matthew 7:8 reads, "Everyone who is asking is receiving. He who is seeking is finding. To him who is knocking, the door is being opened." Jesus restated the same promise, "Therefore I say to you, whatever things you ask when you pray, believe that you receive them, and you will have them" (Mark 11:24).

The answer to the prophet Daniel was sent the day he started asking (Daniel 10:12). It continued while he prayed through three weeks of cosmic battle. Asking is the way you as a branch draw life from Christ, your Vine. Asking itself is an action of faith. It is an expression of confidence that God can and will answer your prayer. Thank God often that His answer is on its way as soon as you begin to pray. It will wonderfully help your faith!

A third step will now lift your faith beyond the future to the God who is timeless.

Step 3: *God Did* Thank Him! Ephesians 1:3

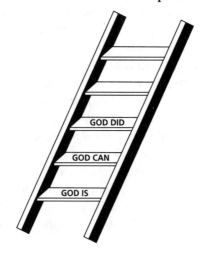

Once we begin trusting God for what He can do, we begin discovering what He has already done for us. This discovery leads to an attitude of gratefulness and thankfulness. Ephesians 1:3 expresses gratitude toward God for His immense generosity. "Blessed be the God and Father of our Lord Jesus Christ, who has blessed us with every spiritual blessing in the heavenly places in Christ."

God is eternal and timeless. He has already accomplished everything He is ever going to do! Actually, God finished His work at creation. That is why He rested on the seventh day (Hebrews 4:4).

God sees everything in time all at once. Two events illustrate God's existence above time.

First, in the mind of God, Jesus was slain before the foundation of the world (Revelation 13:8). In our time, Jesus was crucified about A.D. 33. God is unlimited rather than confined like we are to events in a point of time. God's "clock" is eternal.

Second, to God you were known and chosen before creation (Ephesians 1:4,5). Do you recall the day or evening when you were saved from sin? That was not the moment when God opened His heart to you. He designed and loved you before you were conceived.

God has already prepared answers for all your needs. They are packaged and waiting for delivery when you ask!

Your faith will surge when you realize that God's provisions are waiting for you. Big requests do not send God hunting for solutions. His answers for you have been completed for centuries. It is much easier to believe God for things that you know He has already arranged.

Paul reminds us to pray with a grateful heart, "In everything by prayer and supplication, *with thanksgiving*, let your requests be made known to God" (Philippians 4:6). The readiness of prayer answers compels us to pray with thanksgiving.

To put this aspect of your faith into practice, pray like this: *Heavenly Father, I receive the answer that You have ready for my need. Thank You for holding it in store for this present time and releasing it according to Your perfect design. In Jesus' name, amen.*

Look back at the progress we have made on our Ladder of Faith. First we realize who God is, then what He can do in response to our prayers. To further expand our faith, we learn what He has done for us. Now we go on to grasp what God is waiting for us to do.

Step 4: *God Does*   Obey Him!   Ephesians 3:20

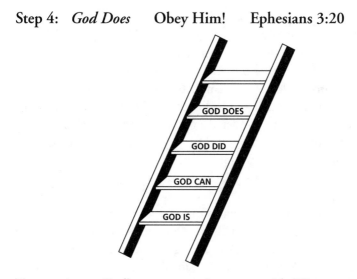

To experience God's power, get into step with His program. Paul addresses God's incredible power in Ephesians 3:20: "Now to Him who is able to do exceedingly abundantly above all that we ask or think, *according to the power that works in us.*"

God is able to answer prayer in amazing ways! Picture a gracious atomic cloud mushrooming above your praying figure. God can do:

Why doesn't all prayer work this way? The answer may be a simple step for you. Inside the prayer explosion is a control device: "according to the power that *works in us*." That power is God Himself. Disobedience, hostility, and unbelief interrupt His working. A breakdown on any step on the ladder will delay the action of God.

Is your faith weak? Check your obedience. Faith and obedience both work through love (Galatians 5:6; John 14:15). To paraphrase an old proverb, "An ounce of obedience is worth a pound of prayer."

Is God's power being hindered in your prayers? Check out possible resistance to the will of God. Listen to the whispers of the Holy Spirit. Mountain-moving faith grows in an obedient heart. The sooner you do what God wants you to do, the sooner faith will flow in your praying.

One more critical step remains on the Ladder of Faith. It is a little like the hatching of a chick from an egg. The chick needs the exercise involved in hatching—pecking, clawing, pushing—to prepare for its first vulnerable hours outside the shell.

Our faith is exercised in praying. Some prayer answers arrive quickly; others require waiting for the proper time. God builds priceless values into our times of waiting *on* or *for* Him. As John writes, "Whatever we ask we receive from Him, because we keep His commandments and do those things that are pleasing in His sight" (1 John 3:22; also note verse 23).

Step 5: *God Will*   Await Him!   1 Corinthians 2:9,10

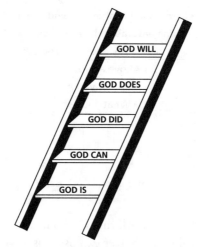

Step 5 on the ladder is the one believers desire most. It is the reason for our praying. When answers to our prayers are delayed, the spiritual lessons we learn are sometimes more important than the answers themselves. "It is written: 'Eye has not seen, nor ear heard, nor have entered into the heart of man the things which God has prepared for those who love Him,'" writes Paul. "But God has revealed them to us through His Spirit. For the Spirit searches all things, yes, the deep things of God" (1 Corinthians 2:9,10).

God delays answers for at least three reasons:

- He takes time to deal with evil forces.

- He takes time to synchronize other parts of His plan.

- He takes time to teach us new truths about Himself.

We explored the first reason for God's delay in answering prayers when we read about the story of Daniel's prayer (Daniel 10:13). The answer to his prayer was delayed because of a battle in the spiritual realm.

The second reason God delays in answering prayer is vividly illustrated by the history of the *JESUS* film. Dr. Bill Bright received a vision for making this film thirty years before it was produced. Believing that the film was a calling from God, he brought the idea before the Lord in trustful prayer. When the answer was delayed, he simply put it on the "back burner" and kept on praying.

Only in recent years have God's reasons for that delay come to light. During the entire time of praying, God was actively forming technology, communications, funding, and staff. When the film was released, an infrastructure was ready for amazing global distribution.

Today the *JESUS* film is the most widely translated film in history. In 1999, it was translated into the 500th language. Outside of the Bible, it is likely the most fruitful tool ever used in evangelism. Distribution continues to expand on an explosive scale. God's delay was part of God's answer! The waiting was essential.

The third reason God delays in answering our prayers is to teach us new truths about Himself. Eternal prayer lessons await people who are willing to wait for the Lord.

Do you have faith steps that need to be strengthened or corrected? First, look back down the diagram and inspect your progress.

Waiting may be the only way you will learn them. You need to listen quietly to the Lord—directly and through other people—to hear His instructions.

Mary and Martha had faith that their Lord Jesus could heal their very sick brother, Lazarus. The Book of John, chapter 11, tells the story. They had probably witnessed many healings during the years they had spent in the presence of Jesus. Believing in His power, they sent a messenger to ask Him to come right away.

Then the Lord Jesus delayed His journey to Bethany and Lazarus died.

What was the response of the sisters when Jesus finally showed up four days late? "Oh, Lord, if only you had come sooner, you could have healed Lazarus! Now it's too late. He's been in the grave for four days."

Here is the beauty of the delayed answer to their request. The sisters believed Jesus could handle illness, but they learned He could also handle death. By waiting, they saw Him raise Lazarus from the dead! Their faith took a tremendous leap up the Ladder of Faith.

You can apply these steps to a major challenge you are facing right now. God has entrusted your challenges to you to feed your faith and help you overcome your world. "Don't quit too soon," said evangelist Wallace Haines of prayer in his day. God will! Await Him! The more you converse with God, the more your faith will grow.

Now that we have a clearer understanding of the role faith plays in prayer, we are ready to tackle another area of living in God's prayer arena: spiritual warfare. As we climb the Ladder of Faith, we get a clearer picture of the battle from God's lofty view. Our spiritual weapons are more effective when we use them with God's perspective.

In our next chapter, we will explore prayer power in winning our battles. Put on your spiritual helmet and draw out your sword. We are heading into another dynamic part of living in God's arena of prayer—spiritual warfare!

Prayerful Response

Lord God, I want to grow in my faith. Many times I have limited You —even insulted You—with my doubting. I confess and repent of my unbelief. Thank You for educating me. Teach me the truths I need to learn about You. Strengthen me to practice the action steps I am learning. In the name of Jesus I pray. Amen.

Personal Reflection

- In what circumstances is God developing your faith these days?
- What steps on the Ladder of Faith could help you grow stronger in faith?
- Why do people often need to redevelop faith, even after God does mighty works?

Practical Step

Share with another believer a faith challenge you are facing. Identify your present position on the faith ladder and indicate the concept of God you need to explore. Review the Scriptures given for your level and discuss ways for you to take the prescribed action step.

Listen to similar information from your friend. Pray for each other and schedule times for mutual checks on your progress.

CHAPTER 14

Winning
BATTLES

RTHUR MOUW WAS a missionary to the big Indonesian island of Borneo. I knew him personally and heard him tell the following story.

Health problems had delayed Mouw's departure to the mission field for several years. His parents used the waiting time, however, as added time to pray for him and the people he would serve. He arrived in the 1930s to serve with the Christian and Missionary Alliance. God gave Mouw and his team a great harvest along the coast. People placed their faith in Christ and were taught to grow in Him. New churches were planted and spiritual awakening spread through the region.

Within a few years, Mouw and his team decided to survey the interior for future expansion. "God has blessed our work here so much," they reasoned, "why don't we take this blessing inland?" They chose the most challenging tribe they could identify—the head-hunting Dyaks.

Selecting a Dyak village on the map, they loaded canoes and journeyed three days up river. As they beached their canoes at the target area, a dark fearful, evil presence attacked them. A strangling sensation left them hardly able to breathe. They gasped out prayers to God for help and pushed their canoes back into the stream.

They reached the main current before they were able to breathe again. The group returned home shocked, defeated, and bewildered.

Mouw concluded later, "I believe we met the Prince of the Dyak tribe that day."

Weeks later, the team began to discern a deep difference between the way they had prepared for their two expeditions. Much prayer had preceded their initial coming to Borneo. Little specific prayer had preceded their Dyak trip. Realizing that missing factor, they called on coastal and home churches to intercede.

Later, when they sensed God was ready, they went inland again. This time God gave them the same kind of harvest they had first found on the coast. A stronghold was captured for Christ and an entire district of churches was established.

On a visit to Indonesia in 1982, I personally saw some fruit from that mission. Substituting for Dr. Ralph Winter, I spoke for an organizational meeting of the Indonesian Missionary Fellowship, a missions association formed to present a united voice to the Indonesian government.

One delegate to the meeting was the superintendent of the Dyak church district. He was a quiet, well-dressed man in his fifties of medium, stocky stature. I was told he was an excellent expositor of Scriptures. As I recall, he said nothing during the conference. He had two unusual marks, however. In each ear lobe was a thumb-sized hole where he had worn earplugs as a cannibal.

That Dyak superintendent had met Christ in the movement led by Arthur Mouw. He was now leading thirty-seven churches in that district because of one previous vital action—Christians had united in serious prayer for lost Dyak people!

Two kingdoms are locked in war—the kingdom of Christ and the kingdom of Satan. Praying Christians get involved in the spiritual battle and invade enemy territory. Christians, having changed kingdoms, are now on the other side of the battle. God is using prayer to wrest territory back from evil control. "He has delivered us from the power of darkness and [transferred] us into the kingdom of the Son of His love" (Colossians 1:13).

Paul Eshleman describes strange, vicious attacks during showings of the *JESUS* film.[1] One incident occurred in a fetid refugee camp in South Africa where people had lost hope. Many were starving and existing in hovels built from any material they could find.

A missionary requested that a Jesus Film team show the *JESUS* film. He had trained the little congregation of forty new believers to counsel the viewers who indicated a desire to receive Christ as Savior.

As the team set up their equipment, people's curiosity began to build. But something was wrong. The team heard witch doctors chanting and saw them throwing bones on the ground in satanic rituals. Paul writes, "With howling and incantations, the witch doctors began calling up spirits of their ancestors. An eerie and foreboding pall seemed to fall over the camp."[2]

This was not the usual experience in evangelism opportunity; this was spiritual warfare. The team and the South African believers began to pray. For three hours they implored God to send His blessing and bind the power of the evil one. They asked that He open the eyes of the people to God's love and truth. As the believers finished their prayers, they joined hands and walked in a circle to symbolize encircling the camp in prayer.

As darkness fell, ragged refugees streamed to the showing area. The witch doctors stopped their chanting. About a thousand men, women, and children crowded to see the film.

During the scenes of the crucifixion, something unusual began to happen. At most showings, a few people will cry when they see Christ's pain and humiliation. Here, however, a mournful wailing rose with an increasing crescendo. Everyone was crying. Eshleman writes:

> Rivers of tears poured down dirty cheeks. Young men, old men, and women beat their breasts and cried out, "Oh, God! Oh, God!" Some were on their knees, some stood with eyes closed and arms raised, others lay prostrate on the ground. The interpreter lay on his back in the dirt, praying, thanking God, crying, praising, worshipping, confessing. Everywhere people were confessing their sins. The film was forgotten. These people were in the presence of a holy God, and they were overwhelmed.
>
> They ignored all the ropes, and huge clouds of dust filled the air as people watching from both sides of the screen rushed to the front.[3]

When the members of the film team tried to pray and counsel with the people, they couldn't speak. They fell on their knees confessing their own sins. For more than thirty minutes, weeping and prayer filled the field. Then someone turned the film back on and the people watched the burial and resurrection of Jesus. When the interpreter explained that death could not hold Jesus in the grave, the crowd exploded into clapping and cheers, dancing and hugging.

The team never had an opportunity to finish showing the film. So many people wanted to receive Christ—in fact every person in the audience—that the counselors were overwhelmed. The following Sunday, 500 new believers showed up to worship in the tiny forty-person church!

With God's power, we can conquer! But how can you and I deal with enemy forces? God has given us a field manual in Ephesians 6:10–18. Four instructions in this passage can prepare you for battles that are sure to come.

Where Are My Supply Lines?

Instruction 1: "Be strong in the Lord and in the power of His might," directs Ephesians 6:10. Supply depots of God are enormous—greater than all satanic forces! But God waits for us to summon Him. In love, He waits to be asked. God's provisions are dispensed from the throne of grace. He longs to mobilize intercessors.

Asking is how you, a branch, draw all the life you need from Jesus, your Vine (John 15:5). He expects you to ask enough for yourself and enough more to produce life-giving fruit for others.

Prayer is not all-powerful, but it connects us with an all-powerful God. A large number of intercessors does not add influence with God. He uses many or few. All prayers are different, however, each designed by the Holy Spirit. More prayers therefore give God more ports of entry into needy situations. Enlist all the intercessors you can.

Finally, to be "strong in the Lord" means to draw upon the total power of Jesus (Matthew 28:18; Hebrews 7:25). You fight spiritual battles by merging your praying with His. You do this when you pray in His name. (See Chapter 10 for the role of Jesus in your prayers.) Persistent prayer is stronger than any other power known to man.

What Protection Do I Need?

Instruction 2: Develop good defenses. "Take up the whole armor of

God" declares Ephesians 6:13. Battle plans changed after Calvary. Satan still has superhuman power, but he has absolutely no power against Jesus Christ and those who live by faith in Him. Christ commissioned Paul "to turn [unbelievers] from darkness to light, and from the power of Satan to God" (Acts 26:18).

The same apostle also prayed that the Ephesian believers would know:

> ...what is the exceeding greatness of His power toward us who believe, according to the working of His mighty power which He worked in Christ when He raised Him from the dead and seated Him at His right hand in the heavenly places, far above all principality and power and might and dominion, and every name that is named, not only in this age but also in that which is to come. And He put all things under His feet, and gave Him to be head over all things to the church, which is His body, the fullness of Him who fills all in all (Ephesians 1:19–23).

God's people are invincible to the degree to which they interact with Christ, their living Head. The devil, however, has a very effective weapon—an extreme ability to deceive. Deceit is his master technique, and he is so skilled that he "deceives the whole world" (Revelation 12:9).

Spiritual battle equipment, therefore, equips you to deal with the cruel cunning of Satan. Look at verse 11 of Ephesians 6: "Put on the whole armor of God, that you may be able to stand against the wiles [schemings] of the devil."

Spiritual armor is largely defensive. It is so important that Paul mentions it both before and after the warfare targets in verse 12. Each piece of armor defends against a certain kind of evil, deceptive attack.

Satan continually assaults Christian soldiers. Small temptations grow into devastating sins. Disciples drift in prayerlessness, then fall away. Leaders yield to pride and eventually disqualify themselves. Prayerless decisions spin into tragic losses.

Continually inspect your spiritual armor as described in Ephesians 6:13–17. Each item defends you against an evil device. Fortify yourself with each piece to match such satanic schemes as these:

Protective Armor	Deceptive Schemes	Corrective Action
Belt of truth	Little lies	Speak the truth in love
Bulletproof vest of righteousness	Tolerated sins	Practice Spiritual Breathing
Boots of outreach	Neglected witness	Take evangelistic training
Shield of faith	Self-sufficiency	Call on the Father
Helmet of salvation	Secular reasoning	Ask for wisdom
Sword of the Spirit	Busyness	Learn Scripture

God's manual tells us to put on *all* the armor. Your natural abilities cannot deflect enemy missiles. Recognize and prepare for them. Each piece of armor is one aspect of Christ's life in you. Ask Him for and receive the defenses you need for each attack.

In Christ Jesus all armor is waiting, sufficient, and ready for use. You are not left on the battlefield alone and exposed. Christ is with you and in you. As Colossians 3:1–3 states, He is our "protecting fortification":

> If then you were raised with Christ, seek those things which are above, where Christ is, sitting at the right hand of God. Set your mind on things above, not on things on the earth. For you died, and your life is hidden with Christ in God.

We grow in battle skills by obedient action. Each time we wield our sword of the Spirit or put on our belt of truth, we become stronger in our faith. We exchange sinful, worldly habits for obedience to Christ. The trade may require time and sometimes pain, but failure to do so is a crafty trap of the serpent.

Paul describes the miracle that takes place as we exchange the old for the new:

> Your old life is dead. Your new life, which is your *real* life...is with Christ in God. *He* is your life...Be content with obscurity, like Christ. And that means killing off everything connected with that way of death: sexual promiscuity, impurity, lust, doing whatever you feel like whenever you feel like it, and grabbing whatever attracts your fancy. That's a life shaped by things and feelings instead of by God.

> It's because of this kind of thing that God is about to explode in anger. It wasn't long ago that you were doing all that stuff and

not knowing any better. But you know better now, so make sure it's all gone for good: bad temper, irritability, meanness, profanity, dirty talk. Don't lie to one another. You're done with that old life. It's like a filthy set of ill-fitting clothes you've stripped off and put in the fire. Now you're dressed in a new wardrobe. Every item of your new way of life is custom-made by the Creator, with his label on it. All the old fashions are now obsolete (Colossians 3:3–10, *The Message*).

Don't you like putting on something new and clean from an exclusive clothing store? Compare this to putting on stained, oily, smelly clothes from a rag bin. The choice is so clear! The results are so different!

Who are My Enemies?

Instruction 3: Scout your enemy so you can see where to hit him. Ephesians 6:12 puts a satellite reconnaissance on your opponent: "Our struggle is not against people, but against rulers, authorities, world powers, wicked spirits" (my translation from the Greek).

Satan, a former archangel named Lucifer, was cast from heaven for leading a mutiny against God (Isaiah 14:12–15). One-third of the angels joined the revolt (Revelation 12:4,7–9). According to Jude 6, these angels are reserved in chains for the final judgment. Some of them are apparently released at times to set up some strong earthly field positions. (Refer back to Ephesians 6:12.) These fallen angels, more than the people they use, are the real targets of our spiritual warfare. Four tiers of them motivate and influence people.

Rulers (empires). Some Bible versions use the term "prince" to describe these evil angels. "You once walked according to the course of this world, according to the *prince of the power of the air,* the spirit who now works in the sons of disobedience" (Ephesians 2:2).

"Prince" is a biblical term for an empire-level ruler. Historic empires with their member nations were guided, ruled, and united by emperors. The term is even used to designate the Messiah (Daniel 9:25).

Daniel 10:20 describes Persian and Greek princes. These were evil, high-ranking angelic beings who fought God in the heavenly realm. They worked in and through earthly government officials.

Imperial evil princes today use masquerades such as Buddha,

Mohammed, Darwin, Marx, and other dead leaders. As missionaries experience in frontier lands, these princes rule masses of people and viciously oppose the lordship of Jesus Christ. Spiritual emperors are a part of your target range. Other levels are parts of larger empires. Our strategy to overcome them is prayer.

Authorities (national governments). The Greek word for "authorities" is used in Romans 13:1. The term refers to national governments with the power of capital punishment and tax collection.

Direct your prayers also toward evil spiritual forces that act in and through hostile national and state officials. The Christian call to confront demonic national authorities is a high priority according to 1 Timothy 2:1–4. Gospel messengers need to respect, but not fear, these authorities. Christ rose above them all in His death, resurrection, and ascension (Ephesians 1:20–23).

World powers (cultural leaders). These satanic beings lead social movements that enslave and destroy oceans of people all around the world. Immorality, drug trafficking, racial hatred, and international crime are examples. The nature and power of these vices exceed human influence. They are supernatural and defy man's control.

Governments are often unable to solve movements of this kind. Churches sometimes become victims rather than conquerors of these forces. Such evil tides call for intervention by our Savior through the prayers of His people.

When Christians pray, they ask for more than destruction of darkness. They plead for the light of salvation for both victims and leaders of darkness. One illustration is found in the former Soviet Union in Eastern Europe. Immediately after a month of international prayer, communism fell, Christian missions were allowed to enter, and a *JESUS* film curriculum began to saturate the public schools. Another illustration is more recent. In 1999, newspapers in America are reporting a nationwide drop in crime during the very time in which movements of prayer are exploding across the nation.

Wicked spirits (local adversaries). Ephesians 6:12 talks of "spiritual hosts of wickedness in the heavenly places." The first three levels of evil powers we looked at were national and international. The fourth kind operates in local neighborhoods and communities. These evil forces are usually the first ones encountered by God's people.

For example, an official refuses to grant a permit for a Christian event. A neighbor starts a malicious rumor campaign. A son or daughter turns against parents and the Christian faith.

Recognize your true foe in such situations. The people are not your primary enemy. Attack the wicked spirit that is influencing their lives. Call on your victorious Christ to deliver those people from their bondage. Connect the authority of Jesus with each situation. Stay with the effort until the enemy yields!

Can you see a spiritual strategy unfolding here? As you pray, trace links between local, national, and international forces. Moderate national leaders, for example, can be driven to extreme measures by local mobs. When that happens, target those local mobs in prayer.

Local hostility, on the other hand, can be fed by national attitudes. A school board may adopt anti-Christian policies advocated by national education leaders. In this case, focus prayer on the national demonic powers behind those attitudes. Work up to the top levels in targeting your prayers. Apply the authority of the Lord Jesus to each level. This is strategic praying. Go for the jugular vein. Destroy enemy supply lines with the supremacy of Jesus' name!

Around 1960, President Suharto of Indonesia attempted to set up a communist government over his nation. Christians, knowing the brutal tactics of Communists, launched a massive movement of intercession. Out of a political crisis that followed, communism was overthrown, a democratic government was established, large numbers of people including entire communities became Christians, and freedom increased for the gospel.

You have nothing to fear if indeed you are wearing the full armor of God. You are connecting the supremacy of Jesus to ramparts of Satan.

Learning to Fire My Weapons

Instruction 4: Mobilize prevailing prayer. Ephesians 6:18 calls you to persevere in your praying. "Praying always with all prayer and supplication in the Spirit, being watchful to this end with all perseverance and supplication for all the saints."

Spiritual action starts in this verse. As discussed earlier, "praying" used here is not an imperative. It is a participle, carrying preceding actions forward. "Praying" in verse 18 explains *how* to perform the previous three instructions: First, be strong in the Lord and His might —praying always (verses 10,18). Second, put on the full armor of God—praying with all prayer and supplication in the Spirit (verses 11,18). Third, wrestle against evil forces—praying with alert endurance for all the saints (verses12,18).

These actions are the prayer equipment that covers the entire field of battle. They ensure ammunition, provisions, and field action for all believers engaged in spiritual conflict.

Field Operations

Every astute military commander knows that certain strategies work best during a battle. Military training molds soldiers to act instinctively using these strategies.

For example, a soldier is trained to obey the orders of his commanding officer no matter how illogical they may seem at the moment. Soldiers are taught not to do their own thinking during the heat of the battle. Even one soldier acting independently will interfere with the coordination of troop movement. If the ten men in the squad do not act uniformly, someone may die needlessly. Obedience is a matter of life and death, of losing and winning. One able commander is the only person who gives the commands because he understands the strategy and the dynamics of the battlefield he faces.

In the spiritual conflicts we face, God is our commander. Our obedience to Him is no less important than for soldiers in a physical war. He sees the scope of eternity. We must depend on Him and obey His commands completely. The orders He gives us in His Word will prevent us from acting outside His battle plan and bringing dire consequences.

The following points are essential prayer strategies that we must follow during spiritual battles:

- *Battle praying means to go on the offensive in Christ,* to attack enemy strongholds by prayer and expose them to Christ's complete victory. Battle praying persists until a fortress surrenders rulership to God.

- *Winning prayer includes asking and receiving God's direction, supplies, power, ammunition, and protection.* It may mean expanding your base of prayer partners to provide sufficient avenues of action for God. It means continuing until you can cast the burden of the battle onto the Lord (1 Peter 5:7).

- *Allow God to choose your battlegrounds.* Don't invite trouble with reckless raids. Remember Arthur Mouw and the Dyak people. Focus your fire on challenges that God entrusts to you. They will be big enough for all the supplies you can seek from Him.

- *Connect God's power by prayer with the evil level confronting you.* Usually, you will start at the local level. Go forward from your starting point to tackle related national, international, and imperial levels. It does little good to wage local wars while higher supply lines continue to reinforce your adversaries. Move up the chain of command.

- *Aim for fulfillment of the Great Commission of Christ.* Do so realizing that your warfare has a controlling purpose. You are rescuing spiritual prisoners of war.

- *Fight as a team.* Soldiers do not win big battles alone. Network with others who are active in the prayer arena. Enlist other prayer warriors.

- *Keep in "radio" contact with your heavenly Father.* Seek His guidance continually (James 1:5,6). Learn spiritual lessons from each conflict. Improve communications and readiness to seize the offensive in Christ Jesus.

A committed soldier is not content to merely win the battle. He does not put down his weapons at that point and go back home. Instead, he now sets his eyes on advancing further into enemy territory. He expects that what he has learned about fighting will aid him in that advance. Winning the battle fuels his enthusiasm for being part of a world-class army.

In Part 4, "Advancing in the Arena of Prayer," we will discover how God gives us everything to advance His kingdom on earth.

Prayerful Response
This prayer illustrates a response to a specific kind of situation. Adapt it to the battles in which you are currently engaged.

Father, you have given all authority in heaven and earth to your Son. I place now before You the denial from our school officials to allow a Christian club on campus. I ask You to change the hearts of our school administration. I ask You, further, to remove hostility from city, county, and state boards of education toward the Lord Jesus Christ. Reveal Your truth to the National Education Association and other groups that influence educators in our country. Give them a spirit of fairness and goodwill toward the Savior. Open the way for students to hear the gospel.

Convict these leaders of their personal need for Your grace. Give them faith to believe in Jesus! Walk me through this prayer process until You have granted the changes You desire. Lead me to others who can fellowship in a sturdy prayer band. Thank You in Jesus' name for all that You are doing now, even through my prayers. Amen.

Personal Reflection

- What is the biggest spiritual battle you are facing at this time?
- At what level did the conflict start?
- What prayer strategy do you think can be most effective?

Practical Step

If you are part if a prayer group, pray for each other's conflicts. Keep in contact with each other to monitor progress. Be alert to praise the Lord for breakthroughs or to intensify intercession for resistant strongholds. If you are not in a group, gather a team of people to start one.

PART FOUR

Advancing in the Arena of PRAYER

Though times seem dark and desperate, God still reigns on the throne of the universe! Never have we seen a deeper, more profound hunger among the people of God for a spiritual revival than we see right now. God is at work stirring the hearts of His people to pray and seek His face. We are getting closer and closer to the turning point.

Henry T. Blackaby and Claude V. King,
*Fresh Encounter: Experiencing God in
Revival and Spiritual Awakening*

CHAPTER 15

Exploring My CELESTIAL HOME

WAR IS A SERIES of battles. Once an army wins a battle, the soldiers occupy enemy territory. They post their sentries and begin planning for the next advance.

Vigilance is necessary after every victory. After a decisive conquest, an army cannot lay down its weapons and forget the contest. An enemy can counterattack and reoccupy the territory. The victory can turn into retreat.

The same principle is true in the spiritual arena. Satan and his legions continually look for a weakness in the Church. He wants to regain territory we have already won and keep us from advancing.

Satan found the Church in America resting its arms not too many years ago. From the days of the Pilgrims to the beginning of the 20th century, American believers fought hard to conquer the land for Jesus Christ. Great spiritual battles were won in prayer. American laws and public institutions were built upon biblical principles. Great awakenings brought millions of people to Christ. Prayer and Bible reading were exercised in our schools. Most of our prestigious universities were founded as seminaries. The frontiers were being evangelized. Christians founded Bible societies, hospitals, and social service organizations. The Church grew in power and in numbers.

Then the Church let her guard down. Christians bowed out of politics, stopped exercising their influence in education, became complacent about living moral lives. As a result, the enemy retook much of the territory the Church had once claimed. Now we must once again fight some of the same battles to regain lost territory.

Experienced military commanders act on the principle that a good offense is a good defense. During World War II, Allied forces kept advancing and pressing forward, keeping the enemy off balance. While advancing, the commanders were concerned about getting too far ahead of their supply line. Without essential supplies like ammunition, food, and fuel, the enemy could counterattack and win an easy battle.

When General Eisenhower's troops were racing across Europe during the last days of Hitler's Germany, American tanks on the front lines began to out-run their fuel supply line. At that point, Allied forces developed a truck convoy called the Red Ball Express to supply the front line. It helped the Allied forces keep going until a port could be liberated that was closer to the front lines.

The starting point of the Red Ball Express was in Normandy, France, where supplies were stockpiled. An endless belt of trucks flowed east. Every kind of vehicle was pressed into service. Divisions were stripped of their transport companies. The trucks delivered their supplies, then swung back west for more. Some convoys traveled between 600 and 800 miles.

This supply line transported an almost miraculous amount of material to the front lines. As city after city was liberated from Nazi occupation by flag-waving Allied soldiers, people who had lived under tyranny now cheered for the freedom brought by the liberating military.

As believers, we too need to be advancing in our spiritual arena. The spiritual tyranny experienced by people today is far beyond anything General Eisenhower's troops met in Nazi-occupied territory. Sinners are trapped, unable to break free from the bonds that hold them fast.

Our enemies are waiting for us to put down our weapons of war and take a rest. They would like nothing better than to hear us say, "Well, I have won spiritual battles in my own life and learned to pray more effectively. I have reached the goal. Now I can take it easy."

Dear friend, we have only begun to see what God can do! Prayer miracles and victories we never imagined we could see are waiting for us! With God's power, the Church is the mightiest army ever assembled. And we are part of the action!

Our supply line is prayer. Without a continuous, fresh supply of power and guidance from God, we become victims rather than victors. But with an adequate supply, we are invincible!

As we go through this last section in our book, we will learn some principles we can apply as we advance in God's arena of prayer. We will explore new territory—our celestial home. We will also discover how to advance our battlefront beyond our personal prayer concerns into larger arenas such as our cities, states, and nation. We will learn how to recruit new troops to join us in our prayer battles and how to equip these intercessors in the most effective way.

As we advance into enemy territory, we will also learn how to join hands with many other believers to develop our own Red Ball Express supply line of prayer. Let's begin by investigating our new home— our celestial place of prayer!

A Picture of Your New Home

When you received Jesus as your Savior, you began to live in two homes—earth and heaven. You were born the first time into your earthly family. Now you have been born again into the family of God. You are a citizen of both worlds (Philippians 3:20).

Your new heavenly home is the biggest one. It is God's home (Isaiah 66:1). It is yours because you are united to Jesus and heaven is where He lives (Ephesians 2:4–6).

But we don't need to wait until we die to visit heaven. Prayer is the airline to our heavenly homeland. We walk heaven's streets and view its wonders each time we fellowship with the Lord. Adjustment to living in our new home will take a lifetime. Don't worry, though, because each day brings a new adventure. Your new life in Christ is a realm of awesome wonders. It combines:

- Angels like horsemen and chariots of fire (2 Kings 6:16,17)

- A supply of every spiritual blessing (Ephesians 1:3)

- His knowledge everywhere (2 Corinthians 2:14)

- More power than you can ask or imagine (Ephesians 3:20,21)

The best explorers of this spiritual homeland are people who keep coming to God in prayer. The longer we walk with God, the more marvels we discover. Our new sphere is not a novelty. It is our primary residence.

Exploring Your New City

Opinions differ on who penned God's letter to the Hebrews, but the author describes the prayer realm in Chapter 12. The best way to describe prayer, the author decided, was to paint a contrast. One of the most spectacular scenes in history was chosen—God's descent on Mount Sinai (Exodus 19:16–24). When we pray (come to God), the writer contends, we come to a scene much more dazzling than blazing Sinai (Hebrews 12:18–21). We do not come to:

- A dark mountain in a firestorm (verse 18)
- An ear-shattering, trumpeting voice (verse 19)
- A terrifying encounter (verse 21)

Rather, prayer brings us into awesome wonders of heaven. Verses 22 through 24 describe our prayer realm:

> You have come to Mount Zion and to the city of the living God, the heavenly Jerusalem, to an innumerable company of angels, to the general assembly and church of the firstborn who are registered in heaven, to God the Judge of all, to the spirits of just men made perfect, to Jesus the Mediator of the new covenant, and to the blood of sprinkling that speaks better things than that of Abel.

Every time we pray, we enter into the throne room of the One who operates the universe. Prayer transports us far beyond the limits of our physical home into the marvels of our heavenly realm. Supporting verses help describe each marvel even further.

We engage universal power. "You have come to Mount Zion," says verse 22. Psalm 110:1,2 gives God's universal position: "The LORD said to my Lord, 'Sit at My right hand, till I make Your enemies Your footstool.' The LORD shall send the rod of Your strength out of Zion. Rule in the midst of Your enemies!" In prayer, we have access to God's ultimate power.

We walk in supreme splendor. Verse 22 speaks of "the city of the living God, the heavenly Jerusalem." Revelation 21:10–27 describes the heavenly splendor in greater detail:

> In a vision he took me to a towering mountain peak and from there I watched that wondrous city, the holy Jerusalem, descending out of the skies from God. It was filled with the glory of God, and flashed and glowed like a precious gem, crystal clear like jasper. Its walls were broad and high, with twelve gates guarded by twelve angels. And the names of the twelve tribes of Israel were written on the gates...

> The angel held in his hand a golden measuring stick to measure the city and its gates and walls. When he measured it, he found it was a square as wide as it was long; in fact it was in the form of a cube, for its height was exactly the same as its other dimensions—1,500 miles each way...The city itself was pure, transparent gold like glass! The wall was made of jasper, and was built on twelve layers of foundation stones inlaid with gems...

> No temple could be seen in the city, for the Lord God Almighty and the Lamb are worshiped in it everywhere. And the city had no need of sun or moon to light it, for the glory of God and of the Lamb illuminate it. Its light will light the nations of the earth, and the rulers of the world will come and bring their glory to it. Its gates never close; they stay open all day long—and there is no night! (TLB).

How amazing that intercessors enter a place of absolute splendor! Who wouldn't want to visit as often as he could? Once there, who would want to leave for long?

We release unlimited action. You are accompanied by "myriads of angels" (verse 22, NASB). Hebrews 1:13,14 says that angels minister to your needs. "To which of the angels has He ever said: 'Sit at My right hand, till I make Your enemies Your footstool?' Are they not all ministering spirits sent forth to minister for those who will inherit salvation?" Although we cannot see them, these angels are engaged in our concerns and battles, releasing God's unlimited action in our behalf. They are swift and numerous.

We enter complete fellowship. Hebrews 12:23 addresses this fellowship as "the general assembly [festal gathering] and church of the firstborn who are registered in heaven." We are not alone. We are joined by millions of believers around the world—the invincible Body of Christ (Ephesians 1:22,23).

We call forth absolute justice. Verse 23 pictures believers turning to "God the Judge of all." Psalm 50:6 trumpets a supreme judicial command: "Let the heavens declare His righteousness, for God Himself is Judge." Intercessors need not fear any injustice we face here on earth. Our citizenship in heaven allows us to draw from a place where all is fair because God has perfect justice.

We follow excellent examples. The end of verse 23 announces that we have spiritual models: "the spirits of just men made perfect." They are further described in Hebrews 12:1,2:

> Therefore we also, since we are surrounded by so great a cloud of witnesses, let us lay aside every weight, and the sin which so easily ensnares us, and let us run with endurance the race that is set before us, looking unto Jesus, the author and finisher of our faith.

These believers have gone on to the celestial city before us. We can look to their lives for encouragement and example. Through their trust in a faithful God, we can be assured that our faithful God will be true to us, too.

We receive a perfect supply. The next verse in this passage acknowledges your Supplier, "Jesus the Mediator of the new covenant." Hebrews 7:25 gives further credence to Jesus' role: "Therefore He is also able to save to the uttermost [completely] those who come to God through Him, since He ever lives to make intercession for them." Our supreme Savior, Jesus Christ, is committed to pray for praying people and thus to supply all our needs (Philippians 4:19).

We enjoy total acceptance. Hebrews 12:24 continues: "...to the blood of sprinkling that speaks of better things than that of Abel." Abel was the second son of Adam and Eve. He and his brother Cain each brought an offering to God. Cain brought vegetables, products of his farming, an offering that God did not accept. Abel obeyed God's command by killing a sheep and offering its blood as a substitute payment for his disqualifying sinfulness. Abel's offering pictured Christ's sacrifice for sin thousands of years later. Hebrews 10:19–22 clarifies our acceptance in Christ:

Therefore, brethren, having boldness to enter the Holiest by the blood of Jesus, by a new and living way which He consecrated for us, through the veil, that is, His flesh, and having a High Priest over the house of God, let us draw near with a true heart in full assurance of faith, having our hearts sprinkled from an evil conscience and our bodies washed with pure water.

The Hebrews 12 passage speaks of your home right now, dear intercessor! This is the realm of prayer! God the Son purchased it for you by the blood of His Cross. God the Holy Spirit brings you here and seals you by His presence in your life. This is the locale in which you meet God the Father in prayer.

Your position in your celestial home is eternal. "Therefore let no one glory [boast] in men. For all things are yours: whether Paul or Apollos or Cephas, or the world or life or death, or things present or things to come—all are yours. And you are Christ's, and Christ is God's" (1 Corinthians 3:21–23). No matter where intercessors go, what they experience, or what they suffer, they are with God, with feet planted in their celestial home. One day we will occupy heaven in person, but right now we have our citizenship secured and visit every time we pray.

The Heart of the Arena

As beautiful as our home is, intercessors do not spend much time gazing on the visual features. Their eyes, instead, are fixed on God. He is the One to whom they are coming in prayer. Heaven, as marvelous as it is, is only a setting for God. His face, revealed in Christ Jesus, captures the gaze of the soul more than all other glories of heaven.

Cosmic wonders do serve a valuable purpose. Do not underestimate them. They exalt the One who sits on the throne. Without these wonders, we might reduce Jehovah's rightful honor to our tiny dimensions. Downsizing God lowers our faith to the same degree. But the wonders of heaven point to God's majesty and glory. That is their purpose.

Visit your heavenly home by coming to God frequently. In worship, explore your heritage in Christ Jesus as outlined in Philippians 3:10,11: "That I may know Him and the power of His resurrection, and the fellowship of His sufferings, being conformed to His death, if, by any means, I may attain to the resurrection from the dead [here and now]."

Gaze on His wonders in secret, with Jesus alone. Come not as a visitor, but as a resident. Tourists enjoy fleeting, but shallow, views of the landscape. As a resident you have the rights and time to explore and mine the wealth that awaits you.

Gazing Into the Stars

The wonder of our dual citizenship is that we can see so many evidences of our Almighty God. They are around us everywhere.

Jim Elliot was one of five missionaries in Ecuador who was martyred by Auca Indian spears. An honors alumnus of Wheaton College, he wrote in his journal a beautiful witness on January 16, 1951:

> I walked out to the hill just now. It is exalting, delicious. To stand embraced by the shadows of a friendly tree with the wind tugging at your coattail and the heavens hailing your heart. To gaze and glory and give oneself again to God, what more could a man ask? Oh the fullness, pleasure, sheer excitement of knowing God on earth. I care not if I never raise my voice again for Him, if only I may love Him, please Him. Mayhap, in mercy, He shall give me a host of children that I may lead through the vast star fields to explore His delicacies, whose fingers' ends set them to burning. But if not, if only I may see Him, smell His garments, and smile into my Lover's eyes. Ah, then, not stars nor children, shall matter—only Himself.[1]

A short while after he wrote this entry, Jim Elliot and several missionary colleagues journeyed to the Curaray River to "lead a host of children...through the vast star fields to explore [God's] delicacies." The desire of his heart was to introduce others to Christ so that they too could gaze past the stars and into God's heaven. There he and his friends met God because of a fatal spear attack—and he gained everything he wanted! Because of the heroic actions of those men and others who followed them to the Curaray River, many Auca people believed in Jesus Christ.

May you also live "to gaze and glory" and give yourself again to God and to smile into your Lover's eyes. Whether we are here or there, we are called to walk and talk with Him!

Prayer Response

My radiant Lord, Your splendor is awesome! You dwell in absolute grandeur. I exalt You now, and give You the highest place in my life—forever. The more I adore You, the more I rise in faith in You. I would cringe in terror to come near to You were it not for Jesus. Through Him I dare to come close. Thank You, my dear Lord Jesus, for washing me and making me acceptable to the Father.

As I come near to You, I come near to heaven's Mount Zion. I take hold of Your power for my weakness. I exchange my earthiness for the majesty of Your heavenly city. I open my prayer list in sight of your vast throngs of dazzling angels. I rejoice in the assembled fellowship of the saints in glory.

I come to You as my beloved Father. I ask You to impart justice and forgiveness to all the people You have entrusted to me. Though I am on earth, I come to You, Lord Jesus, in heaven. You are praying at the Father's right hand. This is Your home. I am one with You. Your home is my home, too.

I do not want to be an occasional visitor here any longer. And so, my Savior, by faith I accept permanent residence here—today. All glory be to You, Father, Son, and Holy Spirit forever! Amen.

Personal Reflection

- What might help you relate your prayers more clearly to the greatness of heaven?

- How might you sustain a more consistent awareness of heaven in your prayers?

- What steps might you take to draw more personally on the resources of heaven?

Practical Step

Individually or in a group, go back and pray your way through Hebrews 12:22–24. Then rejoice before God in the grandeur of this exploration! (Information about praying through Scripture is given in Chapter 11.)

CHAPTER 16

Becoming Part of a Prayer MOVEMENT

HOW IS GOD using prayer today?

In 1987, Campus Crusade for Christ's director of affairs for Eurasia called me from Moscow, Russia. "Can you get Christians to pray for one month for the Soviet Union?" he asked. He explained that the 70th anniversary of the Bolshevik Revolution was the following year.

Christian believers were wondering how to observe seventy years under Soviet cruelty. They decided to set January as a month of prayer for Soviet churches and were asking other countries to join them.

The Campus Crusade prayer office began at once to spread the appeal around the world. Prayer networks, church groups, and conferences responded readily. Eastern Europe broadcaster Earl Poysti recruited prayer across the Soviet Union by radio. Peter Deyneka Jr. brought the Slavic Gospel Association into the effort. The staff from Eastern Europe published a daily prayer guide for the nations.

The number of people who prayed that January is not known, but it appeared to be large. Prayer groups were reported as far east as Sakhalin Island in the Pacific Ocean. A California church, launching their month in a dark rural barn, conducted an "underground" prayer meeting, complete with a mock police raid.

One Russian mayor heard of the prayer movement, phoned a pastor in his city, and demanded, "What are you doing?"

"We're praying," answered the pastor.

"What are you praying for?"

"We're praying for revival," was the reply.

"What is revival?"

"Wait and see," said the pastor.

The mayor did not need to wait long. On the first working day after that month of prayer, Premier Mikhail Gorbachev signed release papers for all religious prisoners across the USSR. Atheistic Communism began falling from power, and the largest spiritual movement of modern times began. Here's how it progressed.

The *JESUS* film was translated into the Russian language. At the Moscow premier of the film, the commissar of education requested copies of *JESUS* for Russian public schools. The Academy of Science and government departments did the same for their personnel.

A consortium of eighty mission agencies united under the banner CoMission. For the next five years, this group trained more than 38,000 public school teachers in the former Soviet republics to use the film. They also learned to use a related ethics and morals curriculum in their classrooms. About 60 percent of those teachers indicated they had trusted in Christ as their Savior during the convocations they attended.

By 1995, the film and biblical curriculum strategy leaped to other countries on four continents under the name Youth at the Crossroads. This ministry began providing Christian AIDS-prevention packages to entire national school systems.

January 1987 was only one of many prayer efforts for the former Soviet Union. But the worldwide prayer rally served to trigger an explosive chain reaction. Prayer among pastors, men, women, young people, and even children has accelerated internationally going into the 21st century. We call this kind of momentum a movement of prayer.

A different story, however, came earlier from the United States of America.

On the Other Hand...

Do all efforts by Christian believers to expand God's kingdom have such far-reaching results? No. We can never determine what God has in store or how He will move among us. But we can be assured that anything we try without prayer will be less effective. Prayer is a universal key.

Around 1890, Pastor Arthur T. Pierson led a remarkable crusade to evangelize the world by 1900. Leaders chose the slogan, "Reach the World in This Generation." Huge strides were made in world missions. The Student Volunteer Missionary Movement sprang up and 100,000 university students answered the call of Christ. Of these, 20,000 went out as missionaries; the other 80,000 stayed home to support them.

A Laymen's Missionary Movement inspired more than 300,000 business and professional men across the United States to support world missions. Even World War I didn't stop this grassroots effort.

Despite the phenomenal gains, Dr. Pierson's crusade did not reach its goal. Extensive areas in Central Asia and the Middle East remained untouched with the gospel. Seventy years later, Dr. Ralph Winter counted more than 16,000 people groups still beyond missionary or evangelistic plans.[1]

Why the shortfall? Dr. Pierson and his co-workers agreed, prayer was not a major emphasis.[2]

In startling contrast, as Christians move from the 20th century into the 21st, a tidal wave of prayer has begun flowing across cities, countries, and continents. Entire prayer ministries and networks have sprung up and multiplied. The movement has exceeded anything like it in history.

Vast advances in world evangelization have followed the explosion of prayer. At the time of this writing, unprecedented gains are being reported in evangelism, church planting, Bible distribution, humanitarian aid, and Christian media. These gigantic gains in prayer, however, only point to a much greater harvest to come. A century-end volume of prayer for the Muslim world is an example. Millions of Christians have been praying for Muslims during several Octobers, the Islamic holy month of Ramadan.[3] Breakthroughs are beginning to occur in that megasphere. But they do not yet match the full scope of the praying.

When you neglect to pray, you may hinder the far-reaching results of God's work in the world. But when you pray, you become part of a movement bigger than your solitary efforts. Like these Christians of times past, your prayers make an eternal difference!

How Can I Best Help My Country?

Prayer has played a decisive role for centuries. Abraham built altars and called on the Lord everywhere he went. By this action he subdued kings and founded the nation of Israel (Genesis 12–15). Elijah turned a nation back to God by his praying (1 Kings 17–18).

Daniel had a custom of praying three times a day. He held his people together through captivity under two world empires.[4] Luke 2:37 says the prophetess Anna "served God with fastings and prayers night and day." At age 84 she introduced the Messiah to the world. Read Hebrews 11 for a giant galaxy of faith that shines with lives of other people who affected history through their praying.

One of the best advancements we can make in God's arena is to join with others in prayer for our country. Bill Bright shares this illustration of the power of prayer on a nation:

> You will recall that the decade of the '60s and early '70s was a chaotic period for America. Many problems beset the United States—the war in Vietnam and resulting conflict in our own country, the radical movement, the drug culture, the racial conflict, disintegration of the home, sky-rocketing crime, an economic recession, loss of military superiority and many others. Some of these problems came as a result of the 1962 Supreme Court ruling which led many to believe that prayer and Bible-reading were illegal in the schools of America. I believe that this action led to our nation experiencing the chastening of the Lord.
>
> But think about what God did. In 1970, shortly after many Christians began to pray for healing in America (claiming 2 Chronicles 7:14), according to the Gallup Poll only 17 percent of the American people believed that faith in God was very important. Yet by 1976, 56 percent believed that faith in God was important—an incredible increase which cannot be explained apart from the miraculous, supernatural power of God.
>
> Furthermore, 85 million people were in church every Sunday and one in five was attending weekly Bible studies or prayer meetings or other religious meetings in addition to Sunday wor-

ship. In less than eight years, a mighty miracle of God had reversed the evil tide which was sweeping America, and a great spiritual awakening was moving in an unprecedented way in the hearts of tens of millions.[5]

"Prayer is out of control," reported C. Peter Wagner in 1996. "Never, since Pentecost itself, has history recorded a level of prayer on six of the continents comparable to what is happening today."[6]

A safe conclusion is that God is preparing an ingathering of people like the world has never seen. Dick Hillis, a former missionary to China and Taiwan and the founder and director emeritus of OC (Overseas Crusades) Ministries, uses the phrase, "Go where the fire is burning and pour gasoline on it." I write to pour gasoline on the fires of God.

God used evangelist Merv Rosell during my pastoral years to keep prayer fires hot in my soul. Here are some poignant comments from his sermons that I carry with me to this day:

> God's most exquisite gift to man—the crown jewel of all His gifts—is the ability to converse with Him in prayer. Christians today are not stuck for money. We're stuck for believing prayer. I want to plead with you to turn from your pulpiteering to your prayer closet. You don't get clean just to get clean. You get clean to go to work. You get clean to pray.

God is all-encompassing and He uses prayer as His vehicle of action. The psalmist forecasts that all humanity one day will come to the God who answers prayer. "O You who hear prayer, to You all flesh will come" (Psalm 65:2).

"The great people of the earth today are the people who pray," writes S. D. Gordon. "I do not mean those who talk about prayer. Nor those who say they believe in prayer. Nor those who explain about prayer. But I mean those people who take time and pray. They have no time. It must be taken from something else. This something else is important. Very important and pressing, but less important and less pressing than prayer. These are people that put prayer first, and group the other items in life's schedule around and after prayer."[7]

Prayer movements require many different kinds of intercessors joining in one effort. Today a deluge of prayer occupations is available for many kinds of gifts. Some opportunities fit young people with adventure in their blood. Some are careers for scholars, authors, or ministers. Some are possibilities for older volunteers who thought their productive years were past.

Consider the following list of prayer roles for those that may be right for you. Appendix G, "Summary of Prayer Positions," also lists these roles so you can easily refer to them later when you are building a prayer ministry.

Individual Volunteers
These volunteers pray for specific requests that are brought to them.

- *Intercessor:* A volunteer who seeks to 1) grow in prayer as a way of life, and 2) pray as the Lord leads, without required structural accountability.

- *Adoptive intercessor:* A person who accepts prayer responsibility for one or more ministries or target areas in the Great Commission of our Lord Jesus Christ.

- *Discipler:* Intercessors who journey into difficult territories around the world for short-term, on-site prayer, and spiritual warfare (often praying while walking through the community).

- *Prayer ambassador:* An intercessor who travels to the scene of a special Great Commission advance and ministers short-term, usually at his or her own expense. He or she intercedes for the special endeavor and disciples local intercessors.

- *Writer/Correspondent:* Intercessors with the gift of communicating spiritual concepts in written form.

Corporate Ministry Volunteers
These intercessors function in groups of praying believers to encourage each other in prayer and to pray according to current challenges facing the ministry they support.

- *Prayer group leader:* An intercessor who accepts an appointment to start and/or lead neighbors or colleagues in prayer for Great Commission goals.

- *Prayer group captain:* An intercessor with administrative ability to assist leaders of two or more prayer groups in:

Recruiting and training new leaders

Forming new Prayer Groups

Supplying prayer materials

- *Coordinator:* A leader who spreads a prayer movement in a church, city, culture, campus, country, or continent.

- *Representative:* An intercessor trained to appear at public events in behalf of an agency, usually in his or her larger residential area. The Representative is able to provide prayer information, materials, encouragement, and assistance to area ministers and Leaders.

- *Editor:* An intercessor with the ability to sort, sift, condense, communicate, and publish material available in today's increasingly voluminous sources of information.

- *Instructor/Trainer:* An intercessor with the ability to teach prayer in classes, conferences, retreats, schools of prayer, workshops, and leadership training classes.

- *Helper:* An intercessor with the gift of serving and helping others generate effective prayer.

Staff Ministries

Funding is an important consideration for the following positions. Financial arrangements for a position depend upon 1) the requirements involved, 2) the available corporate monetary resources, and 3) the individual resources available to the ministering person.

Ministering persons may consider themselves as missionaries and enlist supporting partners in line with the policies of their agency. Parent bodies who benefit from their intercessors should make growing budgetary provisions for developing prayer ministries.

All prayer ministries need to be authorized by a church or agency, according to the doctrinal, administrative, financial, and procedural regulations of that body.

- *Missionary:* An intercessor who makes a long-term move to another location and serves a prayer ministry there. John "Praying" Hyde was an example.

- *Pastor/Minister:* An intercessor who is ordained to the Christian ministry and is called by a church or agency to lead prayer development within that body of Christian believers.

- *Administrator:* An intercessor who can help a prayer team to identify and grasp organizational objectives.

No one can carry the burden of fulfilling the Great Commission
alone. Some, like Elijah or Anna, may carry greater portions than
others. But we all grow through exercise. Every Christian believer
has a vital role in God's spiritual army. When you grow in prayer,
long to share it with others. God is watering that desire like a tropi-
cal rain forest. The more you engage in spiritual warfare, the more
you grow in faith!

How Can I Know God's Will for My Role?

First-century Christians discerned God's will by markers that can
also guide us like harbor lights today. You will find these markers in
Acts 13:1–4:

> Now in the church that was at Antioch there were certain
> prophets and teachers…As they ministered to the Lord and fast-
> ed, the Holy Spirit said, "Now separate to Me Barnabas and Saul
> for the work to which I have called them." Then, having fasted
> and prayed, and laid hands on them, they sent them away. So,
> being sent out by the Holy Spirit, they went down to Seleucia,
> and from there they sailed to Cyprus.

Let me isolate some of the principles given in these verses:

"The church." Explore possibilities with others.
Prayerfully investigate possibilities that are open to you. Author
David Bryant writes of our worldwide battle, "This is no place for
loners. Who else in your Christian fellowship desires fuller involve-
ment in the world mission of the church? Gather regularly with
them for world Christian Bible study and prayer. Help evaluate each
other's gifts, experiences, and strengths in light of current needs and
opportunities. Since God calls us into Body life, He sends us out in
a Body mission."[8]

Listen to the whispers of the Holy Spirit (Isaiah 30:21). Christ
works through His people like your head works through your entire
body. People will usually *misunderstand* God's will if they cannot get
along with God's people.

If you do not have a loving Christian fellowship, ask God to lead you into one. Seek the counsel of mature saints in the body of Christ. Get counsel from a godly pastor or an older saint. No fellowship is perfect, *but find one where Christ can continue His work in you.*

"At Antioch." Build your vision.
God's passion is for the entire world (John 3:16). The believers at Antioch were an international group located in a doorway to the world.

To know God's will, look into His world objectives. Your call to follow your Lord is more important than a call to a particular place. Places may change; His calling is changeless. Expand your Acts 1:8 Personal Prayer Plan with current facts and opportunities, peoples yet to be reached, and ministries God is using today. (See Appendix C, "Personal Prayer Plan Worksheets.") As you follow God's will, He will reveal new steps in His vision.

"Prophets and teachers." Dig into Scripture.
The more you study God's Word, the more clearly you see your place in His world plan. Scripture unfolds His awesome blueprint. Fill your mind with God's Word as a lamp to your feet and a light to your path (Psalm 119:105).

"They ministered to the Lord." Wait on the Lord for guidance, power, supply, and fruit.
"Seek, and you will find," says Matthew 7:7. "This," says Dr. Porter L. Barrington, "is prayer for a knowledge of the unrevealed will of God in a specific need. When you do not know the will of God regarding a need, whether it be material or spiritual, then you are to seek His will in prayer concerning this need to find it."[9]

Focus prayer on unreached people, strategic events, strongholds of Satan, and obstructions. Two valuable byproducts in this prayer agenda are greater sensitivity to God's voice and greater freedom to understand and obey His design.

"Fasted." Fasting helps to subordinate your natural preferences to the Father's will.
Christians in the Bible fasted with their praying because they desired God's will more than their own. (Chapter 17 gives more information on fasting.) You can know God's will only when your own

desires are subordinate to His.

While fasting, make the essential surrender of your will as a loving, living sacrifice. Then start every morning with a grand intention: "I am willing this day to seriously explore new possibilities in God's role for me in Christ's world cause."

"The Holy Spirit said…" Listen to the whispers of the Holy Spirit.
The Spirit resides in your life to reveal the riches that Christ has for you (John 16:14). Obey both His promptings and His restraints. Here are four guidelines to help you distinguish between the guidance of the Spirit and personal ideas:

1. Maintain a personal neutrality before God regarding your decisions.

2. Seek the counsel of older, mature saints.

3. Test ideas with the clear instructions of Scripture.

4. Although there are times to call on the Lord with a loud voice (Acts 4:24), extended quietness is essential to hear the whispers of the Holy Spirit. Isaiah 30:15 records, "Thus says the Lord God, the Holy One of Israel: 'In returning and rest you shall be saved; in quietness and confidence shall be your strength.'"

"Separate to Me Barnabas and Saul." Obey the clear leading of the Lord.
Walking in the light is a key factor in knowing God's will. It means obeying God's instructions to you, which may be costly. The price paid by the church in Antioch was the loss of two top leaders. Yet the church continued, undeterred, through God's supply of their needs. By obeying, they gained the promise of Jesus: "Whoever loses his life for My sake will find it" (Matthew 16:25). You, too, will find that obedience leads to a clearer vision for following Jesus.

"They went." Take the first steps.
You do not—indeed, you cannot—know all future steps in advance. God's total call is often not completely clear at first. Trust God to show you the other steps when you get to them. The two missionaries, Paul and Barnabas, started in the two lands they knew. They first went to Cyprus, Barnabas' homeland, then continued in Paul's country, Turkey. The Spirit took them onward from there.

The other leaders "laid their hands on them." These leaders involved themselves personally with the guidance they sought for outgoing missionaries. Seek this relationship for both sides of the sending/going equation. Do not go forward alone. As the well-known Christian song "Onward, Christian Soldiers" declares, "All one body we."

Another reason for a sending base is that you need to be accountable to an authority. This sustains a sense of responsibility to God. Acts 14:27 continues the story of Paul and Barnabus: "When they had come and gathered the church together, they reported all that God had done with them." They were encouraged by the telling and the church was encouraged by the hearing. At this point, a celebration of God's answers to prayer could have occurred.

Lay out before the Lord these markers from Acts 13. Pray over them like the early Christians did and dare to ask Him to show you the steps He wants you to take. Get counsel from other Christians.

When God's direction becomes clear for your prayer ministry, ask Him to open doors. Accept closed doors gratefully. Investigate opportunities, even if they do not appear to be the kind you expected. These steps, taken together, can disclose the Father's will to you.

Prayer movements are a maneuver in helping to fulfill the Great Commission. They conform to Christ's world-saturation plan as revealed in Acts 1:8. The plan for implementation is revealed in John 14:13,14 and 15:16. As a member of the Body of Christ, your role is essential. God has equipped you with unique abilities to aid in the working of the Body. Prayer movements are inspired by and led by His Spirit. But He will use your role as part of His great plan!

Another avenue that we can use in our prayer role in the Body of Christ is that of feasting and fasting in prayer. Our next chapter will show us how these two opposite prayer activities can benefit us.

Prayer Response

O Lord, my God, I marvel that You might use me in Your world plan. I want to discover Your role for me. Teach me the way I should take. Help me take my first step. Lead me to others who are hearing Your call. Make me burn for You and spread the fire of passion for You. I pray in Jesus' name, amen.

Personal Reflection

- The Spirit of God generates movements of prayer. How do you think God might use you to help generate such movements?

- What might be a good prayer strategy for evangelizing:

  A high school?

  A neighborhood?

  Non-Christian relatives?

Practical Step

Alone or in a group of two or more, identify a country that needs disciples. Recall that Jesus' way to get answers is to pray for them. In your prayer, ask God for enough intercessors *in* or *for* that country to cover the need. Agree to sustain this praying until you can cast the care upon your Lord as directed in 1 Peter 5:7.

CHAPTER 17

Feasting and FASTING

D R. BILL BRIGHT made an unusual announcement in the spring of 1995. "God has impressed me," he told the Campus Crusade for Christ headquarters' staff, "to begin a forty-day fast. The terrible spiritual and moral decline of our country and overwhelming opportunities for the gospel worldwide require His intervention. I may not fast for forty days. I may fast for only thirty days, or ten. But my goal is forty."

Bill Bright's goal became an immediate challenge to me. Shouldn't I, as the ministry's international prayer coordinator, be the first to join him?

Forty days loomed like a Mount Everest before me. Bill's options, however, gave me an escape hatch if I should need it. He might not complete a full forty days. I decided to try.

The fast was a liquid fast, with lots of water and non-acidic juices. Bill and I checked frequently with each other as we carried out normal activity schedules. A big advantage for me was to find more time for praying during mealtimes.

As I fasted, I found that I was more responsive to the Spirit's prompting and guidance. Fasting also strengthened my awareness of God's presence and my longing for fulfillment of Christ's Great Commission.

My fast carried a small amount of discomfort, but it was not very difficult. Even the discomforts reminded me to pray. After four or five days, my digestive system settled into a non-eating mode. At that point, it was not hard to attend a luncheon or banquet without eating because I did not experience hunger.

During the fast, the Lord became exceedingly real to me. Today as a result of those forty days, I am experiencing His presence more than ever. Advances in ministry have resulted. New insights, development, resources, faith, strength, and blending of circumstances are frequent. Heavenly riches were a worthy exchange for short-term sacrifices.

The closing years of the 20th century are witnessing a remarkable resurgence of fasting, most visibly through the influence of Bill Bright.[1] Prayer with fasting is expanding worldwide. Fasting conferences in the United States are gathering tens of thousands of believers annually. Multitudes are participating through televised satellite locations. The movement seems to be preparing Christ's people for His return, as suggested in Matthew 9:15:

> Jesus said to them, "Can the friends of the bridegroom mourn as long as the bridegroom is with them? But the days will come when the bridegroom will be taken away from them, and then they will fast."

Bible fasts and feasts celebrated past achievements. They honored God for blessings of the present and provided instruction for the future.

Both feasting and fasting are biblical exercises and important in the working of God. Both express spiritual values when exercised for God's glory. Each should be observed when the situation is appropriate. The following list compares the different ways we can express ourselves through feasting and fasting:

Feasting expresses:	Fasting expresses:
1. All is well	All is not well
2. Reward	Repentance
3. Assurance	Action
4. Honor	Humility
5. Christ's sufficiency	Christ's Commission
6. Welcome to newcomers	Seeking the lost
7. Praise to the Lord	Seeking His face

8. Thanksgiving	Thirst for God
9. Blessings from God	Birthing His purposes
10. Gratitude for answers	Power for advances
11. Strength	Struggle
12. Peace	Problems
13. God's goodness	God's groanings
14. Delight	Determination
15. Viewing valleys	Scaling summits
16. Savoring the harvest	Preparing for the harvest
17. Fellowship with people	Facing opponents
18. Remembering God's works	Pursuit of His wonders
19. Refreshing our bodies	Weaning our flesh
20. Confidence	Concerns
21. Victories	Battles
22. Celebration	Conquest
23. Cheer	Compassion
24. Hunger for food	Hunger for the Father
25. Today	Tomorrow
26. Basking in sunshine	Reaching for stars
27. Eating the fruit	Feeding the root

The Importance of Feasting

Bible feasts were notable events on Israel's national calendar. *Nelson's Illustrated Bible Dictionary* gives this definition:

> The feasts and festivals of Israel were community observances. The poor, the widow, the orphan, the Levite, and the sojourner or foreigner were invited to most of the feasts. The accounts of these feasts suggest a potluck type of meal, with some parts of the meal reserved for the priests and the rest given to those who gathered at the Temple or the altar for worship. One of the feasts, Passover, originated in the home and later was transferred to the Temple. The rest were apparently observed at specific times during the year and in designated places.[2]

These were the major feasts that the nation of Israel celebrated regularly:

The Feast of Booths or Tabernacles: This festival commemorated

Israel's forty years of wandering in the wilderness when they lived in temporary shelters. The feast was a celebration of God's guidance and supply.

The Feast of Dedication, or Hanukkah, or the Feast of Lights: This festival remembered the cleansing of the Temple after its defilement by Antiochus Epiphanes, king of Syria. It was a celebration of freedom.

The Feast of Passover: The first of three great festivals among the Hebrew people, it recalled the night in Egypt when God's death angel "passed over" houses on which the blood of a lamb was smeared on the doorway. This feast was a celebration of substitutionary redemption. It also pointed forward to the sacrifice of God's Lamb on the cross of Calvary for the sins of humanity.

The Feast of Unleavened Bread: As part of the Passover, it looked back to the haste with which the nation of Israel left Egypt. The required absence of yeast in the observer's bread signified the absence of sin required by a holy God.

The Feast of Weeks or Harvest, or Pentecost: It was during this feast that the Holy Spirit was poured out onto the first Christian believers.

The Feast of New Moon: This observance was an offering to cover sin committed in each previous month. The feast called attention to the human need for forgiveness and cleansing.

The Feast of Purim or "Lots": This celebrated the deliverance of the Jewish people from destruction during the time of Queen Esther. This feast proclaims God's deliverance of His people from evil today through prayer, trust, and obedience.

The Feast of Trumpets: It was a week of self-denial, cleansing, renewal, and expectation. Christians see in this solemn festival an allusion to preparations for the Second Coming of Christ.

Feasting carries dangers along with its value as a celebration of God's goodness. Debauchery and desecration often displace godly purposes. Christians in England in the Middle Ages became so riotous that the Puritans outlawed observances for a number of years.

In modern times, Christians utilize several feasts for potential spiritual value. I use the word "potential" because often our excesses eclipse our quest. The Christmas celebration, for example, commemorates the coming of God to earth as a baby. Often it becomes focused on gift giving or receiving rather than on the precious gift of

God's Son. Easter celebrates Christ's resurrection from the dead. At times, even believers turn the celebration into a time to hunt for eggs or dress up in new clothes. Thanksgiving gives praise to God for His bountiful blessings upon us. How often do we exchange our thankful attitudes for those of gluttony or merely reveling in family fellowship?

Prayerful feasting is illustrated today by the Jewish Seder (Passover) and the Christian observance of the Lord's Supper, also referred to as the Eucharist, Communion, or Holy Communion. A pause for prayer is related to each element of the menu. Churches and families who keep the spirit of these feasts use these occasions for instruction, worship, and joy. Spiritual and physical health can be improved by seasoning our diet with more prayer. Silent or audible, interspersed prayer can lift us above our animal appetites and keep our attention on the One from whom these table blessings are flowing.

One Bible verse can guide God's people in feasting as worship. "Therefore, whether you eat or drink, or whatever you do, do all to the glory of God" (1 Corinthians 10:31). A strong prayer life is needed to observe this rule—whether at Christmas, an award dinner, or any other occasion.

Fasting has become a much rarer discipline in modern times. For that reason, we will focus attention on fasting in the rest of this chapter.

The Importance of Fasting

God also used fasts in the lives of His people throughout the Bible. Fasting offers several benefits for times of need:

- *Fasting is a biblical way to intensify prayer.* Fasting helps to clear the mind and body for God's use.

- *Fasting helps us transfer our attention from the material world to God.*

- *Fasting strengthens faith.* A weakening of the body is a qualification for power in prayer. "When I am weak," said Paul, "then I am strong" (2 Corinthians 12:10).

- *Fasting and prayer deepen our seriousness about spiritual realities* (Matthew 16:24).

- *Fasting can strengthen us to deal with human oppression and need.*

A supreme goal of fasting and prayer is to grow in faith and in fellowship with God. As He becomes more important to you, you are happy to invest the time and means necessary to "cast your care upon Him" (1 Peter 5:7). A description of fasting is given in Isaiah 58:6–8:

> Is this not the fast that I have chosen: to loose the bonds of wickedness, to undo the heavy burdens, to let the oppressed go free, and that you break every yoke? Is it not to share your bread with the hungry, and that you bring to your house the poor who are cast out; when you see the naked, that you cover him, and not hide yourself from your own flesh? Then your light shall break forth like the morning, your healing shall spring forth speedily, and your righteousness shall go before you; the glory of the Lord shall be your rear guard.

Isaiah teaches us that fasting must be motivated by love, not by tradition, liturgy, spiritual pride, or manipulation. We should fast for:

- *Authority to remove chains of evil* from our life, loved ones, and country
- *Power to lift sickness, suffering, and sin* from the lives of people
- *Hearts of mercy* to clothe the naked and give bread to the hungry
- *Compassion for fellow Christians* who suffer persecution for their faith

Will Fasting Results Surprise Me?

Fasting with prayer produce two kinds of supernatural developments. The first kind is *when heaven comes down.*

Anna was an old widow who served God with fastings and prayers in the temple most of her life. Because of her heart attitude in fasting and prayer, God showed her the infant Christ (Luke 2:36–38). Another example is Cornelius, a Roman centurion in Israel, who was fasting and praying when an angel told him to send for Peter (Acts 10:30–32). As a result, he and his family were saved and baptized.

The second kind of supernatural development is *when hell breaks loose.* Do not be surprised or afraid if intensified prayer arouses Satan. Despite evil opposition, God gets His work done. Nehemiah, fasting and praying for his home city, received a commission to return and rebuild it. Enemies later harassed and tried to interrupt the workers, but the work was completed in a remarkably short time (Nehemiah 1,2).

After fasting for forty days, Jesus was tempted and taunted by the devil in the wilderness (Matthew 4:1–11). He went on to conquer Satan at Calvary. Paul, who fasted often, went to Rome as a prisoner and suffered shipwreck on the way (Acts 27:43,44; 2 Corinthians 6:4,5). Through it all, Paul contributed thirteen books to the New Testament.

Fasting with prayer gets God's work done. Fastings are decisive battles. Paul assures that "in due season we shall reap if we do not lose heart" (Galatians 6:9). While fasting, keep the victory of Jesus in view. Advance in the authority of His name.

When Should I Fast?

Five basic situations call for fasting and prayer. The first is *when you purpose to honor God's law of rest.* By adding a fast to a day of rest, you experience the benefits of a much more complete kind of rest (Isaiah 58:13,14).

A second situation is *when you need to humble yourself before God.* You see this in Jonah 3:5,10: "The people of Nineveh believed God, proclaimed a fast, and put on sackcloth, from the greatest to the least of them…Then God saw their works, that they turned from their evil way; and God relented from the disaster that He had said He would bring upon them, and He did not do it."

A third instance is *when you face humanly impossible situations.* David models this humility in 2 Samuel 12:22,23. He said, "While the child was still alive, I fasted and wept; for I said, 'Who can tell whether the Lord will be gracious to me, that the child may live?' But now he is dead; why should I fast? Can I bring him back again? I shall go to him, but he shall not return to me."

Another time for fasting and prayer is *when you need God's guidance for decisions.* The Antioch church leaders turned to God for direction in Acts 13:2,3: "As they ministered to the Lord and fasted, the Holy Spirit said, 'Now separate to Me Barnabas and Saul for the work to which I have called them.' Then, having fasted and prayed, and laid hands on them, they sent them away." The event marked the birth of a missionary era.

A fifth circumstance is *when you need healing from a serious affliction* (Isaiah 58:8). When the disciples asked Jesus how He cast an unclean spirit out of a young boy when they could not, He replied in Mark 9:29, "This kind can come out by nothing but prayer and fasting."

You also see prayers for the healing of a nation in Daniel 9:3–5:

> Then I set my face toward the Lord God to make request by prayer and supplications, with fasting, sackcloth, and ashes. And I prayed to the Lord my God, and made confession, and said, "O Lord, great and awesome God, who keeps His covenant and mercy with those who love Him, and with those who keep His commandments, we have sinned and committed iniquity, we have done wickedly and rebelled, even by departing from Your precepts and Your judgments."

What Kinds of Fasting May I Choose?

The Bible does not command us to fast or even prescribe the type of fast to observe. The kinds of fasting and their duration are therefore left to our own spiritual hunger and burden. A variety of options are open to you.

Time periods for fasting in the Bible include three days and nights, one week, many days, and forty days (like the fasts of our Lord Jesus and Moses). Fasts fall under three categories.

First is the *typical fast*. The Bible teaches that normal fasting means completely refraining from solid food. The typical fast did not involve abstinence from liquids. Matthew 4:2 reports that Jesus was hungry after fasting for forty days and nights. It does not say that He was thirsty. Scholars believe that Jesus drank water in the wilderness but did not eat food.

Second is the *complete fast* or *absolute fast*. This is a severe fast that involves no food or water (Acts 9:9). A person should not go on a complete fast, as a rule, for more than one day.

Third is the *partial fast*. This fast is marked by restrictions on the type and frequency of food eaten. Daniel 1 states that Daniel and his friends drank only water and ate vegetables. They abstained from meat and wine from the king's table. You might call this type a "Daniel fast." On several occasions John Wesley ate only bread when he fasted.

The partial fast may involve a specific time period. Options include daylight hours, a full day, or just one meal at a time. This kind of fasting may also include abstaining from marital intimacy as mentioned in 1 Corinthians 7:5.

Korean Christians have made prayer and fasting a priority since the late 1940s. Today the church in Korea is growing at a phenomenal rate. For decades their practice of fasting has been a factor in an annual church growth rate of 10 percent and a national military that is more than 50 percent Christian.

What Guidelines Should I Follow?

Jesus taught His people that fasting has no reward if it is done to impress people. Fasting is not designed to get the eye of the world but to get the ear of God! "Moreover, when you fast, do not be like the hypocrites, with a sad countenance," says Matthew 6:16. "For they disfigure their faces that they may appear to men to be fasting. Assuredly, I say to you, they have their reward." Fasting helps God's people to intensify worship, intercession, and advances against evil strongholds.

Jesus further warned about pride in fasting. He illustrated the point with a Pharisee who stood in the temple and thanked God that he was not like other men. The Pharisee boasted, "I fast twice a week" (Luke 18:12).

Another danger is legalism—the effort to gain merit with God by good works. Fasting does not generate favor from God. His total grace is freely given to us in Christ Jesus (Romans 5:21). When a person places his trust in fasting for salvation, fasting then becomes as Titus 3:5 says, "works of righteousness which we have done." No such works can save us.

Some people try to equate spirituality with fasting. Actually the Bible does not tell you how long or how often to fast. The Bible does not give a standard formula for fasting. Follow the leading and burdens of the Holy Spirit. Spirituality comes from the heart, not from physical performance. Also, do not compensate for your fasting with later lustful indulgence. Always do your fasting for the glory of God (1 Corinthians 1:31).

For further reading on fasting, two books will be very helpful. Dr. Bill Bright has written of his fasting experiences in *The Coming Revival*. Dr. Bright also offers other resources on how to undertake a personal fast or conduct a fasting seminar. (See Resources in the back of the book for ordering information.) Also, a booklet titled "How to Plan Forty Days of Prayer and Fasting," published by the Evangelism and Home Mission Association of the National Association of Evangelicals, is available by contacting NAE at P.O. Box 50434, Indianapolis, Indiana 46250-0434; (317) 570-5125.

History shows us that God's power can work in miraculous ways in advancing the gospel of Jesus Christ nationally and even globally. Feasting and fasting in prayer can begin this process. Other strategies can also allow us to become part of God's plan for the centuries.

Great spiritual harvests are occurring in many parts of the world. Revival is sweeping many lands! As you learn more about God's arena of prayer, you too can discover more prayer strategies that will make the enemy shudder.

Prayer Response

Holy Father, teach me to enjoy spiritual feasting as much as physical feasting. Teach me to balance physical appetites with increasing spiritual hunger. Thank You for providing prayer with both feasting and fasting for Your people. I confess to You my strong leaning toward sensual feasting. I need the discipline of self-denial, for my appetites sometimes conflict with my love for You. Although fasting does not appeal to me, I long for a life more conscious of You! Help me to grow in prayerful feasting and fasting. In the name of Jesus, amen.

Personal Reflection

- Have you engaged in prayerful feasting or fasting? Describe one of your experiences.

- How might fasting help your prayer life?

- What are some conditions in our times that call for fasting and prayer?

Practical Step

Plan a noon hour or an entire day to fast and pray. Identify one or more objectives for this period. Pray your way through a Scripture related to your goal. Follow an A-C-T-S procedure dividing your time for Adoration, Confession, Thanksgiving, and Supplication (asking). Record your experiment in a journal. Make your time a loving adventure with your Lord!

CHAPTER 18

Developing Prayer STRATEGIES

THORLIEF HOLMGLAD was a pastor in downtown Oslo in the 1930s. It was a depressing spiritual time in Norway. One Sunday evening when he stepped down from the pulpit, he was met by an excited church custodian.

"Pastor," the custodian exclaimed, "there's going to be a revival in this church!"

"Revival?" Holmglad asked. He motioned his hand toward the many empty seats. "Does this look like revival?"

"Come with me," said the custodian as he beckoned Holmglad behind the pulpit. "Do you see those water marks in the carpet? Those are tear stains. I have been praying and weeping here for five years. The Lord has assured me He is going to send a revival!"[1]

In a nearby city around that same time, two women also began praying for God to send a revival to Norway. "Lord," they prayed, "if this burden is from You, will You send two more women to pray with us?"

He did. The four asked the Lord successfully for four more, and the eight for sixteen. The growth stopped at that point.

God answered their prayer on a Sunday evening in a church youth meeting. The group was restless. The leader tried in vain to get their attention. As the meeting struggled on, the leader saw something like a white cloud descend slowly from the ceiling. He was the only one who saw it.

The lower it came, the more restless the youth became, until the cloud touched the tops of their heads. Instantly, without any outward signal, all the youth fell to their knees praying, weeping, and confessing their sins.

The teenagers carried that spirit into the evening worship service. Adults fell to weeping in penitent prayer. They returned to church Monday evening and throughout the week, bringing others with them. The brokenness of spirit remained, and the revival continued for twelve years!

Revival spread to other churches in the city, then to other cities throughout the country. During those twelve years, twenty thousand people were converted and added to the churches in Oslo alone. This revival prepared the nation for the dark years of Nazi occupation.

Young people, gripped for God in that atmosphere, eagerly offered themselves as missionaries to other lands. For decades Norway sent more missionaries abroad proportionately than any other country.

Lutheran pastor Armin Gesswein traveled from New York to observe, then to preach in the Norway revival. He met his lovely wife, Reidun, during those days. He gave the rest of his life to promoting revival throughout the world. Mary Jean and I have been personal friends of the Gessweins for nearly fifty years.

Seven Prayer Principles for Revival

What can we learn from this historic account in Norway? Is there something we can apply to our own area? Seven spiritual principles burst from the Norway revival.

- *Revivals grow out of prayer movements.* Spiritual harvests in turn grow out of revivals.

- *Prayer movements begin with one or two fervent intercessors.* These people stand in the gap between a sinful land and God's wrathful judgment (Ezekiel 22:30).

- *Intercessors follow the burden of their heart.* To intercessors, anxieties are a call to prayer (Philippians 4:6,7). God calls them to help accomplish His plan.

- *Burdens have an ending point.* The goal is to pray until you can cast your burden on the Lord (1 Peter 5:7). You then rejoice in the peace of assurance. Remember the Oslo custodian's prophetic announcement: "Pastor, there's going to be a revival!"

- *Answers may assume unusual forms.* Ask God for discretion to recognize and willingness to receive His way of doing things. Consider characteristics of the Norwegian church youth meeting in terms of Isaiah 55:8–11:

    "My thoughts are not your thoughts, nor are your ways My ways," says the Lord. "For as the heavens are higher than the earth, so are My ways higher than your ways, and My thoughts than your thoughts."

- *Answers will exceed your asking or imagination.* Their size is worth the wait (Ephesians 3:20).

- *Revivals need space.* Do not restrain invasions of God. Instead, recognize what God is doing. Suppose that the youth leader had given up and dismissed the youth service. Or suppose that Pastor Holmglad had closed the church for succeeding meetings. Change plans if needed to help revival happen!

Several of these principles were present during a movement of the Spirit that I witnessed recently. Revival seized Campus Crusade for Christ in 1995. United States staff members were holding a biennial conference at Colorado State University. Nancy Leigh DeMoss spoke to four thousand people about the need for brokenness before our Lord.

Following the message, master of ceremonies Chuck Klein made an unusual announcement. In a choked voice, he said something like this: "God has spoken to me this morning. He may have spoken to many of you. I am going to take a seat on the main floor. If any of you want to share what God is saying to you, you may come forward and say it to the rest of us."

Lines of people began to form at two aisle microphones. Staff members shared confessions, repentance, and testimonies in tearful brokenness before God. After each expression, fifteen to twenty people rushed forward to surround and pray for that individual. For twenty-five hours over the next three days, seminars, meal times, refreshment breaks, and even plenary sessions were set aside. It was an unprecedented time for a staff conference. The revival became a deep, thorough, supernatural cleansing from God, which resulted in Campus Crusade for Christ experiencing new spiritual growth and harvest.

God used two revival essentials to prepare the leadership for that conference. First, *God used a prayer priority.* For fifty days, Campus Crusade's headquarters personnel had prayed and fasted for the staff conference. They asked God to set aside the planned program, if necessary, to accomplish His plan. His answer was awesome.

Second, *God used flexibility.* When God's Spirit began moving, Campus Crusade's president Bill Bright and the program committee set aside a well-planned schedule. They paid a heavy price to make room for the Holy Spirit. Though all honoraria were paid, many major speakers did not give their presentations.

Urgent priority was given to God. Crowds forgot their meals in the university cafeteria. Ministry leaders met in tearful prayer in a final session and signed a covenant of spiritual renewal.

How Can I Help Increase Spiritual Harvests?

God's Spirit works in fresh ways in times of revival like those in Norway and Colorado. We find ourselves with a whole new mind-set, one that focuses more clearly on God. What a blessed experience that is!

To be used of God for revival of small or large proportions, we must examine the prayer power that precedes these revivals. We must ask ourselves: What can I specifically pray that will bring me closer to God's heart for my church or area? What form should my prayers take to focus them on the need at hand?

Christ used four overall objectives to stir the first Christians to prayer. They are found in Acts 1:8: "You shall receive power when the Holy Spirit has come upon you; and you shall be witnesses to Me in Jerusalem, and in all Judea and Samaria, and to the end of the earth."

His objectives led to a watershed prayer meeting that launched the Church Age. They are ideal targets for every ministry. Use them to plan goals for your praying. They include:

1. Your local area   (Jerusalem)

2. Your county, state, province, country   (All Judea)

3. Your mission fields   (Samaria)

4. A frontier God has for you   (End of the earth)

Just as in our individual prayer plan, we can use strategies to help us strengthen our praying for revival. The women in Norway had a specific plan—to ask God to increase their small group of intercessors. God brought the people He prepared to their group.

Revival not only brings spiritual renewal to the hearts of believers, it inspires desire to help fulfill the Great Commission—Christ's command to all His people. One way to fortify our prayers is to focus on a spiritual harvest. The following suggestions will help you align your praying with God's heart of compassion and His power. These five crucial prayer strategies will inflame your prayers for the Great Commission. They are practicable, possible, and potent as commanded in 1 Timothy 2:1–4.

Targeting.

The Bible teaches "goal praying." Scriptures call God's people to ask generously, specifically, expectantly. Jesus was specific in His prayers. So were Paul and John in their New Testament letters.

Aim your prayers at specifics of the Great Commission, using Acts 1:8 as a guide. Build an inclusive prayer plan for yourself and propose one for your church or ministry. Sample worksheets for a church or ministry prayer plan are provided in Appendix F. These Prayer Adoption Registers can be used for enlisting intercessors in your church or ministry, or can be adapted for use with your Personal Prayer Plan.

Mobilizing.

Invite everyone you can to pray for spiritual awakening resulting in spiritual harvests. In his call, the prophet Joel included leaders, youth, children, couples, and pastors (Joel 2:15–17). Today people increasingly want to find a place in international prayer. Thousands of prayer networks are growing rapidly. You, too, can play a vital role! Do not allow difficulty to deter you. Be flexible in tactics, but keep pressing toward the goal. Chapter 19 will give more information on how to recruit prayer warriors.

Matching.

No individual alone can pray for "all men" (1 Timothy 2:1–4). Ask intercessors to adopt specific prayer targets, as well as domestic and foreign prayer needs of their church or organization which God lays on their hearts.

Campus Crusade's Global Adoptive Prayer program matches adoptive intercessors with specific areas of the world. Every volunteer is encouraged to pray for a slice of his or her own country, then to intercede for a region in a less-prayed-for land. It is a plan by which any Christian can take spiritual responsibility for their portion of the Great Commission. Other agencies have similar ways to match people with global opportunities. Contact the ministry God lays on your heart or contact your church's denominational prayer office to match your praying with needy areas of the world. Chapter 21 provides a list of addresses and telephone numbers for many of these agencies.

Communicating.

Relay news of results to your intercessors. Look for a prayer correspondent—an important new position in Christian ministry. A person in this role serves the Great Commission much like war correspondents do in military conflict.

Paul was a classic prayer correspondent. His letter to the Colossian Christians tells of three others: Epaphras, Tychicus, and Onesimus (Colossian 1:7,8; 4:7–9). Prayer correspondents transmit needs for prayer and news for praise. (See Appendix H for a job description of the Prayer Correspondent.) Five simple rules will maximize the quality of each prayer detail. Each item should be:

- *Urgent.* Intercessors are giving valuable time, so convey requests that are worthy of their time. Emphasize significant issues and report outcomes.

- *Timely.* Write while the action is hot. Information that arrives after an event wastes time and expense and discourages interest. Interest can also decline if prayer appeals are made too far ahead. One month is about right for lead time. Long-term prayer interest can grow even more if big-event needs are divided into a series of short-term needs.

- *Appropriate.* Reserve local requests for local intercessors. Circulate big prayer requests in international circles. Put yourself in the place of people receiving your prayer sheet. Ask yourself, "If this material came to me from another country, would it motivate me to pray?"

- *Broad.* Use prayer information that brings out the big picture. Avoid minutia. Keep your data level significant. Time required for thoughtful communication will yield vital strategic prayer.

- *Brief.* Delete unnecessary words. Get to the point. After all, you are asking people to pray, not to wade through tedious reading.

Prayer correspondence takes time, skill, and patience. But your rewards are changes in the hearts of people and changes in your community and world which advance the Great Commission. In *Operation World*, Patrick Johnstone declares:

> Our prayers change our world, open closed doors, make resistant people receptive, put down and raise up leaders and extend the kingdom of our Lord Jesus.
>
> That fire we pray down mobilizes his Church, calls out labourers, empowers them for the ministry, and brings in the missing disciples from peoples not yet represented before his throne (Revelation 7:9,10).
>
> Is it any wonder the enemy would do all he can to distract or dismay us from commitment to intercession? Let us mobilize prayer! We can tip the scales of history. Christians can be the controlling factor in the unfolding drama of today's world.[2]

Celebrating.
People rejoice when they learn of the workings of God. Prayer celebrations can:

- Glorify the God of the entire universe

- Encourage prayer warriors

- Attract new intercessors

- Launch new initiatives for God

One kind of celebration is to rejoice over answers to prayer. Match the size of the celebrations with the size of the answers.

Another opportunity is to celebrate the completion of intercessory times. Annual or semiannual celebrations can give transforming encouragement to praying people. These observances recognize faithful prayer warriors and enlist new ones. For more help on how to conduct these celebrations, you may order material on Campus Crusade's one-day seminars called "Building Prayer Churches" and "Building Praying Ministries." Write to The Great Commission Prayer Movement, 100 Lake Hart Drive, Dept. 2800, Orlando, Florida 32832-0100, or call (407) 826-2829.

Many years ago, four young men who were burdened for people all over the world met for a prayer meeting under a haystack. That Haystack Prayer Meeting is considered by many church historians to be the beginning of North American foreign missions. They were just a handful of praying believers, but what an impact they had!

Jeremiah Lanphier began a prayer meeting in a small, struggling church in downtown New York City. The response was not very great at first. But the prayer meeting caught fire and began a spiritual awakening that brought more than a million to Christ. One man dedicated to prayer changed American history!

God's Spirit is moving once again in great movements of prayer. It is time for all of us to participate in the most powerful group on earth—people who pray!

God has given us many unique prayer opportunities today. Your heart for His cosmic panorama of prayer can spread out beyond your prayer closet into your corner of the world. In our next chapter, we will learn how we can enlist many more warriors in God's spiritual army.

Prayer Response

Lord, an urge is stirring in me. I long to contribute to revival and world harvest! I have heard that You are breaking out in revival movements today. I worship You for dynamic, new initiatives like fasting and prayer, months of prayer, and the National Day of Prayer. Thank You for awakening churches and colleges, for empowering ministries like Promise Keepers and the Pastors' Prayer Summits. I praise You for stirring youth in many lands! Show me the part I should take. Teach me where to start. I pray in the name of Jesus. Amen.

Personal Reflection

- God does wonders in revivals. How sincerely do you and your acquaintances want a spiritual awakening?

- Why do revivals usually start with brokenness over your own sins?

- Do you think Christian people today might object to a true revival? Why do you think so? What kind of preparation might be helpful?

Practical Step

One method of praying involves groups of three people (triplets) who pray together. Use the following activity with two of your praying friends or with your prayer group. Assign a number to each person in the triplet. Provide three local prayer requests. Ask person number one to pray for one minute for the first request. Ring a bell after one minute, then ask person two to pray for the second request, and number three to pray for the third.

As time permits, move on to state and national needs and pray in the same manner. Rejoice together in the actions of the Lord through these prayers.

CHAPTER 19

Recruiting Prayer WARRIORS

P RAYER IS LIKE HISTORY. Just as making history is greater than reading about it, praying to your heavenly Father is more important that reading books about prayer. And mobilizing others to pray is more strategic than one person praying alone.

God can use you to recruit intercessors! Nothing could be of higher importance. *But how*, you ask, *can I go about something like that? Where would I begin? Am I qualified to be a prayer leader?*

Four actions can help you to enlist new prayer warriors. The letters that start each word form an easy acrostic to remember. They are P-O-L-E: Planning, Organizing, Leading, and Evaluating. You may not personally enlist an army, but you can recruit one or more people who may recruit others. Your influence can expand through them to people you have never met. God is the Lord of the harvest. He knows how to fit you into His plan. Think big and start small. Trust Him to direct it all.

Planning: How Can I Develop Prayer for God's Will in the World?

I have led several prayer tours to the Holy Land. Our goal was to inspire intercession by visiting sites where prayer events occurred. The prayer experiments were exciting, and we hope to try them again.

We have discovered three methods, however, that are more productive than those tours. They are: God-sized world goals; Bible studies and conferences on prayer; and prayer journeys to sites that people adopt for intercession.

God-sized goals are offered in books like *Operation World* by Patrick Johnstone.[1] This book is a daily prayer guide to praying for the world.

Bible studies on prayer are increasingly available in Christian bookstores. Prayer conferences invariably bring intercessors to the surface. Among the many available are five through Campus Crusade for Christ.[2] They include:

- Change Your World Through Prayer and Fasting
- Building a Strategic Prayer Movement
- Understanding Prayer
- The King and the Dragon (spiritual warfare)
- Birthing Spiritual Movements (churches and ministries)

Prayer journeys amplify an identification principle found in Joshua 1:3, "Every place that the sole of your foot will tread upon I have given you, as I said to Moses." You can pray with far greater realism for a frontier, for example, that you have actually visited than for a faceless mass of unknown people. Campus Crusade's ministry, The Macedonian Project, offers prayer journeys to areas of the world closed to open evangelism.[3]

Christ's global witness plan from Acts 1:8 includes all three of these methods. His action plan is also a prayer plan for the harvest. It is summarized in His call to disciples found in John 15:16. He chose us and appointed us to: (1) go and bring forth permanent fruit; and (2) ask the Father for that fruit.

Christ is giving us a strategy. Begin by planning for the harvest in your praying. Prayers are a prime driving force in world evangelization. As we read in 1 Timothy 2:1–4, mobilizing prayer is the very first part of our call to service. The fact that prayer is our connection with God makes prayer basic to Christ's plan. Great Commission prayer as recorded in Matthew 28:18–20 draws four totalities from God: all power, nations, instructions, and time.

To plan a complete prayer menu, use the four fields of Acts 1:8 in the Church Adoption Prayer Registers. Refer to the sample prayer planning worksheets in Appendix F.

Organizing: How Can I Recruit Others to Pray?

A second task for prayer leaders is to enlist other intercessors. It is a necessary way to get things done for God. The choice for every person who is serious about the Great Commission is prayer or push, God or flesh, strength or struggle.

"Does anyone really think that America today is lacking preachers, books, Bible translations, and neat doctrinal statements?" asks Jim Cymbala, pastor of the Brooklyn Tabernacle in New York City. "What we really lack is the passion to call upon the Lord until He opens the heavens and shows Himself powerful."[4]

Prayer strategies still work! Nepal was a closed country when Adon and Mannu Rongong, a Nepalese couple, met Jesus. They fell in love with Him, trained in the Asian School of Theology, then returned home. Only about five hundred Nepalese were Christians at that time. Evangelizing was illegal in Nepal in 1985, so they started to pray. Mannu soon organized seventy national women's prayer groups.

People started turning to the Lord. Within fifteen years, Christians numbered five hundred thousand, and the king canceled laws that hindered evangelism! God has used prayer cells throughout the Church Age, as He did in Nepal.

- When Christ ascended to heaven, all He left on earth was a prayer meeting.[5]

- The gospel entered Europe through Lydia's prayer band (Acts 16).

- Paul started churches as prayer cells. (See 2 Corinthians 1:11; Ephesians 6:18; Philippians 4:6,7; Colossians 4:2,3.)

- Praying house churches are dynamically spreading the gospel today in countries with limited access to Christianity, according to national Christian leaders.

Prayer cells can begin with as few as two people. Four steps will help us to recruit people to pray:

1. Identify God's goals.

2. Subdivide the goals into faith-sized targets.

3. Enlist individuals and cell groups to adopt those targets.

4. Keep those units informed of results.

Organize your intercessors into a network of prayer cells. Feed information to them about prayer needs and prayer news. Teach intercessors to obey directions from the Lord. Then encourage them in winning the battle!

Leading: How Can I Encourage Others in Prayer?

International staff members of Campus Crusade for Christ developed a national prayer model in Russia. They enlisted intercessors to adopt each of the country's three hundred areas populated with one million people. The staff monitored and reported monthly news and needs to these intercessors.

Consequently, a tremendous interest in God and His Word took root in the public schools. Cooperative action by eighty mission agencies, called the CoMission, has served that open door. They have trained more than 38,000 public school teachers to use a Christian curriculum in their classrooms. Of those teachers, 23,000 have placed their faith in Christ. International Christian educators have been mobilized to assist and mentor those teachers. In Russia, the *JESUS* film is being shown nationwide, churches are being planted, and Bible schools are starting!

God's basic prayer strategy is to train leaders. It is the law of the Shepherd (1 Peter 5:1–4). Praying leaders inspire praying people.

Encourage your church and ministry leaders to build prayer into their leadership. (Refer to Appendix F for suggestions.) Share success stories, tools, and methods for developing intercessors. Assist them in building daily personal prayer support teams. (See Appendix K for information on how to build a prayer team.)

Spreading prayer produces a spreading spiritual harvest! Continually seek Christians who are gifted for a variety of prayer ministries. Disciple them in Christ for roles they can fill. (Appendix G provides a summary of potential prayer positions.) Intercede for your disciples. Provide training opportunities, encourage initiative, and inspire creativity. Stand alongside each intercessor as a sincere player-coach.

Evaluating: How Can I Inspire Prayer Passion?

I urge you to regard the recruitment of prayer warriors as a high priority in your ministry. Every army needs fresh troops. Prayer movements require an increasing desire to seek God's face.

Begin with your family. Many prayer warriors received their best training by participating in prayer with their parents or other close relatives. Your Christian friends are a great resource. They can catch your enthusiasm as you share your burden and vision for prayer and the answers you receive.

Don't forget to influence those in your ministry area. If you teach children, model prayer to them. Talk to their parents. If you work with adults, begin by sharing your prayer burden for the ministry area in which you serve. If you sing in the choir, think of it as a base for enlisting intercessors.

The following two strategies can help you establish your prayer warriors in their desire to seek God's face.

Prayer Correspondent

News of answers to prayer fans the flames of prayer. The better the reporting, the stronger the blaze.

Prayer correspondents are a much-needed kind of communicator. They retrieve, sift, and report answers to prayer. The work takes time, labor, and modest amounts of money. However, it is this kind of investment that God uses to walk a movement through to completion (Ephesians 1:15–19). Review the job description in Appendix H. This vocation may be just the one for you or for someone you may enlist.

Situation War Room

Robert Waymire was a U.S. naval officer with access to the Pentagon war room. Every conceivable military situation is played out there with maps, computers, charts, and descriptions. *Every church and mission agency needs a situation room like this*, he reasoned. Goals, graphs, and results on its walls and computers could provide a flow of inspiring material for intercessors. It could be an enormous aid for prayer, planning, monitoring, and communications.

Spiritual war rooms are becoming standard equipment for prayer leaders. See Appendix J for a description of ways to set up your own war room. Talk to your leaders about establishing one for your church or ministry. Make a spiritual war room a center for spiritual action among your intercessors!

Of course, one of the greatest opportunities we have to recruit prayer warriors is to influence our church to pray. In the next chapter, you will read about exciting changes that happen when local congregations commit themselves to pray. As you complete the Practical Step in this chapter, begin asking the Lord to show you how He can use you to build a praying church.

Prayer Response

Lord Jesus, I want to make prayer my primary work in life. Teach me to live in the stellar range You have given to prayer. Help me, heavenly Father, to inspire others to pray for Your burdens until You lift them. Keep our vision on goals and victories that You will give us in Your arena. Spirit of God, use me to recruit intercessors. Breathe on others through me the Spirit of grace and supplications. I give myself to You for this high calling. Through Jesus Christ, my Lord. Amen.

Personal Reflection

- People are attracted to big visions. Do you think this is also true of prayer?
- How might you influence other believers to catch a vision for prayer?

Practical Step

Pray over the Summary of Prayer Positions given in Appendix G. Ask the Lord to guide you in narrowing down the ministries to which He may be calling you. One of these ministries may be His lifelong choice for you, or one may draw you for the present with the possibility of another one in the future.

Your "narrowing" process may sift down to more than one. Hold all options open before the Lord. He will make them clear in His time.

Start making plans to begin your ministry. Seek mature Christian counsel. Keep your heart open and obedient to God's preparation, timing, and training.

Share your exploration with a praying friend. Challenge that friend to become part of God's expanding prayer movement in your church and nation.

CHAPTER 20

Building a Praying CHURCH

C HURCHES SHINE forth in God's world prayer plan. Jesus made that fact clear by an announcement recorded in the first three New Testament Gospels: "My house shall be called a house of prayer for all nations…" (Matthew 21:13; Mark 11:17; Luke 19:46).

Praying churches are central in God's arena. Paul's priorities for churches are startling! Prayer heads the list—before evangelism and other ministry. Paul crystallized church prayer for Timothy, a young pastor he mentored. You see this in 1 Timothy 2:1–4:

> Therefore I exhort *first of all* that supplications, prayers, intercessions, and giving of thanks be made for all men, for kings and all who are in authority, that we may lead a quiet and peaceable life in all godliness and reverence. For this is good and acceptable in the sight of God our Savior, who desires all men to be saved and to come to the knowledge of the truth.

Church prayer may catch fire suddenly, as in a revival. Or it may rise through patient, diligent labor, like building a beautiful house. Both kinds of prayer grow through planting and cultivating seasons. Let me give you some examples of praying churches, from the past and in the present.

The Welsh Revival
I recall the late J. Edwin Orr telling a story from the 1907 Welch

Revival. An Englishman drove his carriage to Wales to observe the revival. He asked at a corner store if the noted Evan Roberts might be preaching that night. The clerk did not know.

"Oh," said the visitor. "I thought a revival meeting might be scheduled somewhere."

"Oh yes," replied the clerk. "There is a revival all right. There will be a meeting in every church, and every church will be filled. But we don't know where Evan Roberts is preaching. We don't know who is preaching anywhere. What we do know is that God will be there!"

The Welsh Revival was a prayer revival that occurred within traditional churches. The Spirit of God simply breathed on well-known Bible truth and set it afire.

This same pattern occurred across the Atlantic Ocean years later.

The Brooklyn Tabernacle

Leap forward 64 years to a depressed community in Brooklyn, New York. An amateur pastoral couple, Jim and Carol Cymbala, reluctantly moved into the pastorate of the dying Brooklyn Tabernacle. In desperation, they made Tuesday night prayer meetings the cornerstone of their work.[1]

Twenty-five miraculous years later, with a membership of 6,000, the church is making a deep local and national impact. Strikingly, the first twenty-five years of cultivation did not merely *lead* to revival. They were themselves revival years of expanding prayer, evangelism, discipleship, sending, and rejoicing!

Wherever churches pray, marvels occur from the hand of God. Among thousands of churches that could verify this statement, I will describe three I know fairly well. Two are located in an East Coast city. The third is 3,000 miles away on the Pacific Coast.

First Baptist Church of Orlando

First Baptist Church of Orlando, Florida, started 1999 with a twenty-four-hour chain of prayer. New life in the congregation blooms under the ministry of Pastor Jim Henry. Decisions for Christ are a normal weekly occurrence. Ninety-one people made life commitments for Christ on a single Sunday early in the year. More than sixty of these were first-time salvation decisions. About that same time, a "Power Lunch" for men resulted in forty-four professions of faith, plus another twenty-four inquiries.

As one might expect, the chain of prayer has continued. Every day is covered by up to fifty-five people. New members are encouraged to sign up for a place on the chain. The church pastoral staff have daily prayer partners. The church is using a widely sung theme, "We've a Story to Tell to the Nations."

Calvary Assembly of Winter Park

Church prayer has financial implications. Calvary Assembly of Winter Park, Florida, carried a mortgage of $11 million in 1996. The church launched a debt-reduction campaign, "Move the Mountain," with a month of round-the-clock prayer.

By March 1999, an amazing $8 million had been received. Prayer became a standard part of church life. Prayer coordinator Alex Zanzanian reported, "Individuals are praying and a sense of God is growing in the services. We are realizing more and more that there needs to be prayer!"

Zanzanian acknowledges that the larger body still lacks an awareness of a need for prayer, but leaders are proceeding to build prayer through small, strategic prayer groups. These groups include a core of fifty to sixty praying people, a missions prayer band, intercessors who pray for more extensive issues, and an "agape group" who pray during church services. A telephone prayer line is always open for requests from the public.

The Church on the Way

Pastor Jack Hayford of Van Nuys, California, is a man of prayer. The church has reflected that influence since he became pastor in 1969. From the beginning, Hayford emphasized prayer as a part of life.

"It was a learning process," reports Dr. John Amstutz, professor at The King's College and Seminary and long-time member of the congregation. "We prayed for the nation. Later we prayed for the nations!" The Church on the Way grew from eighteen members in 1969 to 9,300 (5,000 active members) in early 1999.

The church's Wednesday night prayer meetings keep growing with an average attendance of 700 adults and 500 youth and children. Despite the increase, the church does not see prayer primarily as a church-growth principle, but rather as a kingdom-growth principle. Two examples illustrate this view.

California experienced a serious drought in 1977. Pastor Hayford preached on the spiritual significance of natural disasters from the Book of Joel. The congregation prayed for rain. The winters of 1977 and 1978 each brought a season of unusual rainfall.

In the 1980s the church began to intercede for issues related to crime. Gang activity and the homicide rate were high in the San Fernando Valley where the church is located. In the months that followed, former gang members began a ministry of gang interdiction. The homicide rate dropped dramatically. One year, the police department reported no gang-related homicides![2]

A Deep Foundation

I served as a pastor for twenty-eight years, so I can speak sympathetically for thousands of pastors. We pastors have often wondered: *Where does my congregation fit into God's global picture? We preach the Word. We have prayer meetings. Our bills are being paid. We are a busy people. Those churches in Wales and Brooklyn are in a different league.*

We have no desire to be big. We have an outreach now and then. We lose some members and gain some, and we are showing some growth. We're not a perfect church, but we are happy. We are trying to be faithful. Isn't that enough?

Every church today has the same Master. God is simply waiting for us to call upon Him. He wants us to build praying churches that are great churches—regardless of size.

A praying church is built on a two-layered foundation. The bottom layer is God's *power;* the upper is His *plan.*

The Lower Foundation: God's Power

Like a skyscraper, a praying church begins by deep attention to its foundation. Jesus laid out our foundation in John 15:16: "You did not choose Me, but I chose you and appointed you that you should go and bear fruit, and that your fruit should remain, that whatever you ask the Father in My name He may give you."

The Vine, Christ Jesus, is the root from which we bear multiplying fruit. John 15:5 stresses the point that He is our life. "Without

Me," He said, "You can do…" *quite a lot,* we are inclined to think. "Nothing!" He says. Many times we think we can accomplish quite a lot without prayer. An average church calendar trumpets this concept loudly.

Realistically, the way you regard prayer is the way you regard God, for prayer is communicating with Him. No other way exists in which to relate with Him! Put simply, low levels of prayer signal a demotion of God in our attitude. High levels of prayer indicate an expectation for a fullness of His presence and power.

The Upper Foundation: God's Plan

A church is built on Christ, the bedrock foundation, and God's plan for the church. I wrestled with this part of the foundation as a pastor. *How can I find God's plan for the church He has called me to shepherd?* I wondered. In those days, I was favored to learn of Armin Gesswein and the Revival Prayer Fellowship. At some immensely inspiring pastors' conferences in Pacific Palisades, God saturated my spirit through men like Paul Rees, Bob Pierce, Dick Halverson, Frank Mangs, and Thorlief Holmglad. Seasons of prayer unveiled the throne of God in heaven.

Then I would come back to the cold waters of my church. The chill was not the fault of the people; it was mine. I did not know how to bridge the chasm between the conferences and the church. I write these pages to help pastors who find themselves in a similar dilemma.

If you are a pastor, I urge you to seek God for the plan He has uniquely designed for you. I have included some ideas in this chapter. Digest them in prayer. Integrate His plan into the souls of your leaders. Ask them to help teach and lead your congregation in the plan He unfolds to you.

No single resource can give you all the answers for your church's prayer potential. A single chapter can address church prayer only in a limited way. Principles from earlier chapters of this book apply to churches as well as to individuals. Use the principles you have learned so far as tools to build prayer in your congregation. Many fine books are available on the subject. (See the Bibliography.) Above them all is the Bible itself, our best guide for church prayer.

No prayer movement can succeed unless its leaders are fortified through prayer. One of the most important steps in building a pray-ing church is surrounding you as the pastor and other directors in prayer. The Pastor's or Director's Support Team is designed to pro-vide leaders with a foundational block of prayer that can be used to launch all activities of the church, including movements of evangel-ism and discipleship.

Ideally, the pastor or director selects thirty-one men who will join with him as prayer partners for a given day of each month. If thirty-one men can't be selected, begin with the number of available men and ask them to pray more than one day each month. For example, if you enlist seven men, they will pray one day each week. Appendix K gives more information on how to start and maintain prayer support for ministry leaders.

To motivate and sustain congregational prayer, use the following four operations: targeting, adopting, nurturing, and celebrating. While these practices do not require ideal conditions, they do re-quire diligent shepherds.

Operation 1: Targeting
Start with the questions: What are the scriptural goals of our church? Where do their boundaries lie?

Prayer defines a church's harvest capacity (John 15:16). Paul laid out a huge prayer assignment to Pastor Timothy in 1 Timothy 2:1,2:

> Therefore I exhort first of all that supplications, prayers, in-tercessions, and giving of thanks be made for all men, for kings and all who are in authority, that we may lead a quiet and peace-able life in all godliness and reverence.

Acts 1:8 outlines your church's conquest capacity:

Jerusalem is your local sphere. Your congregational Jerusalem in-cludes three categories: geographical, relational, and functional. They are the neighborhoods, social spheres in which your people move, and activities of your flock such as participation in schools, busi-nesses, social causes, and so forth.

Judea is the larger area in which your Jerusalem is located. Your Judea area is much bigger than your Jerusalem. It includes your city, county, state, and country.

Judea is too immense for one church to cover alone. Neighboring churches also share responsibility for your Judea, so adopt the parts that touch the lives of your people. Plan *saturation* prayer for those parts. Aim for displacement of opposing demonic forces and the release of "fruit"—the people God wants to save!

"All who are in authority" are included: executive, legislative, and judicial branches of government. Notice that prayer produces tranquil, godly lives that are essential for getting the gospel to every person.

A church's mandate requires thorough prayer for all of these fields. Sample adoption registers are presented in Appendix F to help church leaders think through and identify their target areas.

Samaria covers cross-cultural areas served by your missionaries. Samaria's culture was different from Israel's. Jesus used special awareness, skill, and timing to communicate with this people group. Samaria represents your mission fields.

Missionaries need prayer beyond the usual, "Lord, bless the missionaries." Ask your missionaries for their goals for this year or even the next six months. Request information on their ministry opportunities, hostile conditions, and financial staffing needs. Consult material from missionaries and the library on the fields your missionaries are serving. Relate these insights to the targeting of prayer for your Samaria.

The ends of the earth speak of an unreached frontier the Lord is entrusting to you. Praise the Lord that the number of mission frontiers is rapidly decreasing! More and more mission agencies are entering societies that have had no knowledge of Jesus. Your church is needed to help complete the task. Your frontier may be a people group in a territory one of your missionaries is serving.

How do you pray for an unreached people? Intercession is the first step in penetrating pioneer territory. God alone can subdue satanic strongholds where these people live. Therefore, spread out your prayer targets to include:

- Preparation of hearts for the gospel
- The calling and preparation of messengers
- Provision of people to support the invasion financially
- Evangelistic materials, tools, and events
- Provision of linguists and translators

- Favor with the government, media, and community leaders
- The raising up of national disciples and shepherds

Operation 2: Adopting

A strategy question arises: Where will you find people to pray for all of your targets? Two steps are necessary: enlisting and matching.

Enlisting. Church spiritual growth can be expected to the degree in which worshipers are enlisted for prayer. A church has four potential sources of praying people—individuals, families, groups, and the congregation.

Use sermons, studies, discussions, and group presentations to invite everyone in the church to pray. Make the endeavor a special all-church challenge for all ages, including the children. Teach your prayer plan and explain the reasons behind the emphasis on prayer.

Preach on the specific Acts 1:8 goals of your church. Relate united saturation prayer to the release of God's power. Apply the concept of a praying church to every individual, family, Christian education class, committee, and social group.

Designate two annual periods for prayer on the church calendar: February–May and September–mid-December. Avoid the busy summer and Christmas seasons and use January for an annual prayer conference.

Matching. Plan a special event for adopting various prayer targets. Reserve large target fields (such as your state and nation) for the congregation as a whole. Assign second-level targets to groups such as Christian education classes and interest groups. Spread the rest of the prayer areas among participating worshipers and families.

Schedule an adoption sign-up occasion for a Sunday evening or even a morning service. It's imperative for everyone possible to attend. Therefore, design a big event that is significant for all, including youth groups. Distribute material in advance to familiarize people with available prayer options. Provide a nursery with outside attendants so all mothers can attend. Plan attractive music and a program that lead up to a stirring biblical message.

Place large, colorful, well-marked poster-boards around the assembly area beforehand. Or prepare clipboards with the same information. On each one, list a different Acts 1:8 target field for your church. (Put "Our Jerusalem" on one and "Our Judea" on another and so forth.) Provide spaces for people to sign their names next to a prayer target. These sign-up sheets will match each person with a target field for a three-month adoption. Each target space should present a dual goal: one for your church and the other for a wider Acts 1:8 item. (See samples in Appendix F.) It may be wise to begin with two Acts 1:8 areas—your Jerusalem and your Judea. The others can be added as the church grows in prayer.

During the adoption event, the pastor invites the congregation to begin circulating the clipboards. He points out the locations and the format of the sign-up sheets. Prayer is offered to God and the people proceed to sign up for the targets of their choice.

The people may shop around briefly among two or three boards. Each person signs up to pray for one local and one distant target field. Encourage your people to visit the spiritual war room you have set up. (See Appendix J for details on how to create and maintain a spiritual war room.)

The moment of decision arrives after the message. The occasion concludes with a dedication prayer and hearty song of bountiful praise to the Lord. Church goals are now undergirded with intercession and permeated with the power of God.

Operation 3: Nurturing

Prayer is like a plant because it needs care. Nurturing is a normal part of church ministry—in Christian education, home fellowships, or discipling. Spiritual information includes mentoring and Bible teaching on prayer. Initial enthusiasm for prayer will evaporate without the nurture of spiritual and reporting information. The pastor takes the lead in passing along prayer insights.

Reporting information involves news of results. People wonder: *What is happening because of our prayers?* If outcomes are unknown, the praying people will assume that nothing occurred. This view leads to discouragement and distrust in God!

A well-written news sheet will go far in publicizing prayer information. Appoint an editor and encourage the congregation to notify that person of answers received. Prepare a team of reporters with well-placed "news beats," to use a newspaper term. Keep the periodical filled with:

- News of answers for which to praise God (Psalm 50:23)
- Needs for intensified prayer (Acts 12:5)
- Nuggets of scriptural and literary encouragement (Psalm 119:50)
- Testimonies and interviews from prayer experiences (Psalm 39:3)

The pastor is best fitted to lead the charge, sharing general prayer updates in the worship service. Class and committee chairmen fill a similar role at the group level. Every praying church will need a prayer coordinator to maintain a prayer information flow, keep records current, and report to the pastor. In Appendix I, you'll find a suggested job description. Reports of answers will inspire the people. Unanswered issues can call the congregation to intensified prayer.

Assign someone the responsibility of keeping the spiritual war room up to date. If the room remains unchanged for long periods of time, people will lose interest.

Operation 4: Celebrating

Who wants to be part of a gloomy enterprise? That stereotype has tragically tormented church prayer meetings. One reason is that prayer is regarded either as a duty or a badge of spiritual accomplishment—both marks of the Pharisees' attitudes.

Heaven is a magnificent, eternal prayer meeting. The Book of Revelation trumpets this truth in blazing splendor. Church prayer on earth should reflect, however dimly, that kind of glory.

Therefore, churches need to celebrate prayer landmarks such as answers to prayer and testimonies of God at work. When you celebrate prayer, you celebrate God who is the source, means, and goal of your praying. Celebrating prayer is praise set on fire! It is richly biblical. Bible celebrations flowered in feasts, festivals, and memorials.

"Rejoice in the Lord always," Paul charged the Philippians 4:4. Then he reinforced the appeal, "Again I will say, rejoice!" Four kinds of celebrations can strengthen godly praise in praying churches.

First, *celebrate big answers to prayer as a congregation.* Nehemiah tells us, "The joy of the Lord is your strength" (Nehemiah 8:10). All prayer is to be saturated with thanksgiving. Praise is essential to congregational health. Answers to prayer raise joy to the source.

Match the level of your celebrations with the size of your victories. Answers to the prayers of a whole congregation should be celebrated when all people possible are present. Use the same formula for classes, committees, prayer groups, and families. As Psalm 50:23 declares, "Whoever offers praise glorifies Me; and to him who orders his conduct aright I will show the salvation of God."

Second, *celebrate the enlistment of new intercessors.* Create a special interest in your growing spiritual army. Intercessors are priceless. When they are underrated, unnoticed, or unheralded, prayer itself is depressed.

Just as you ask God to send world missionaries, ask Him to raise up spiritual missionaries. When He does so, praise Him with strong celebrations! Celebrations like this can encourage your present intercessors and inspire new ones to step forward.

Third, *celebrate completion of a prayer campaign.* The Bible's Book of Esther is, in large part, the story of Jewish fasting and prayer in a horrifying time. The victory celebration brought praise to God, but also caused many national citizens to become part of His people.

> In every province and city, wherever the king's command and decree came, the Jews had joy and gladness, a feast and a holiday. Then many of the people of the land became Jews, because fear of the Jews fell upon them (Esther 8:17).

Prayer campaigns address major issues, such as public danger, financial crises, and new advances for the gospel. Build faith, joy, and participation with celebrations that are appropriate to the workings of our mighty God!

Fourth, *celebrate each new year.* How fitting to start a calendar or fiscal year by praising God for His grace in the past. Scriptures teach us to celebrate His goodness and mercy. His faithfulness in the past builds our trust in Him for the future.

The New Year is well positioned to honor God for His attributes. Emphasize the qualities of His nature. Praise Him with musical instruments, as David did. Pull out all the stops. When you celebrate the New Year, celebrate God!

Discuss with your leaders the possibility of scheduling a week of prayer. The first week of January was once known widely as Universal Prayer Week. God unusually revived His people during a Universal Prayer Week in Sweden, giving birth to the Evangelical Mission Covenant Church denomination. How different is that story from our traditional frolic that features short-lived New Year's resolutions. It would be marvelous to resurrect this prayer tradition. Honoring this week for prayer can set a pace for the year, give opportunity to enlist new intercessors, and encourage the people in prayer.

Celebrate in your congregation with the closing words of the Psalms, "Let everything that has breath praise the Lord. Praise the Lord!" (150:6).

Church Prayer Escalade

Prayer Escalade is a new prayer strategy for churches. The word means the scaling of a fortified wall during an assault. It expresses a conquest of challenges that God entrusts to a congregation from time to time. Several questions will help us understand the role of an Escalade in the life of a church.

Why should we attempt this advance? God has committed Himself to praying churches. Scripture speaks to the intent of His heart:

- "Is it not written, 'My house shall be called a house of prayer for all nations'?" says Mark 11:17 (quoting from Isaiah 56:7).

- "Call to Me, and I will answer you, and show you great and mighty things, which you do not know," declares Jeremiah 33:3.

- "Though we live in the world, we do not wage war as the world does," says 2 Corinthians 10:3,4. "The weapons we fight with are not the weapons of the world. On the contrary, they have divine power to demolish strongholds" (NIV).

- Ephesians 6:10,12,18 remind us, "Finally, be strong in the Lord and in his mighty power...For our struggle is not against flesh and blood [people], but against the rulers, against the authorities, against the powers of this dark world and against the spiritual forces of evil in the heavenly realms...Pray in the Spirit..." (NIV).

What are we asked to do? Listed on a Prayer Escalade Worksheet are opportunities for people to adopt a church ministry in prayer. (See Appendix L, which includes a worksheet for individual Escalade volunteers and a worksheet for a churchwide Prayer Escalade.) "Adopt" means to accept prayer responsibility for that part of church life. Each volunteer's goal is to pray God's will into action for the ministry he or she adopts.

The church staff appoints a Prayer Coordinator (see Appendix I) who will keep prayer volunteers informed of prayer concerns and church needs. The Prayer Coordinator lists appropriate prayer requests, answers, and other information on "adoption cards" that he gives to each volunteer.

Provide copies of "My Prayer Escalade" worksheet for prayer volunteers. Also adapt the "Church Prayer Escalade" worksheet and post it on a convenient place for volunteers to see and to sign up for prayer areas. After volunteers have been enlisted, provide a copy of the signed roster for your Spiritual War Room.

No specific prayer time is required for volunteers. They agree to pray daily as the Lord leads. They may include this prayer effort in their normal personal prayer time. Participation will help volunteers grow in prayer.

What are we to pray about? The Prayer Coordinator supplies prayer volunteers with information each month and notes spiritual progress. The Coordinator also shares answers to prayer for which to thank the Lord and challenges for which to intensify prayer. This information is obtained from the adopted ministries.

How long will our prayer adoption last? New Prayer Escalades will normally occur during the spring and fall, avoiding the interruptions of summer vacations and Christmas holiday activities. At the end of each period, prayer volunteers should discuss three questions:

1. How has God used this assault?

2. Shall we launch a new one?

3. What changes could be beneficial?

The pastoral staff plan celebrations for big prayer victories.

What if several people want the same target? The ideal plan is to cover all prayer targets first before doubling up. However, if several people are led to adopt one target, let the Lord's will be done. We see this in Acts 5:29 when Peter and the other apostles declared, "We ought to obey God rather than men."

How do we get started? Once the Prayer Coordinator has been appointed and the materials are ready, church leaders announce a meeting to circulate a list of church prayer targets. In the meantime, church leaders pray for the Lord's guidance for each participant. Second, at the meeting each person will have an opportunity to volunteer to pray for one or two important church objectives. Third, each volunteer will receive a "prayer adoption card" that lists prayer details and requests concerning the ministry or area he or she signed up to pray for and the "My Prayer Escalade" commitment sheet.

What if we forget to pray at times? Simply pick up and go forward. Keep your adoption card in a convenient place as a reminder.

What if we receive no answers? That will not happen unless you harbor unforgiveness in your heart. Some results, like sprouting seeds in a garden, may not be visible for a time. Scriptures on your adoption card will keep you trusting and thanking God as a *faithful* Creator.

What if we aren't sure we can keep going for three months? You are right! None of us can. That's why a Prayer Escalade will be an adventure! "It is God who works in you to will and to act according to His good purpose," says Philippians 2:13 (NIV). He who motivates you to start will just as surely energize you to finish. When you pray you are getting in line with Christ's primary desire for His Body.

Prayer volunteers all have reason to pray for one another during this assault. Weekly praise reports will remind everyone to pray for each other. As each person participates, anticipate a season of miracles!

Moving Forward

Does your church today need to rebuild a life of prayer? Can your church re-emerge as a praying army? Be encouraged by the following letter, which Dr. Bill Bright wrote to the Campus Crusade for Christ family on December 23, 1998:

> A Hubble telescope scientist announced a few days ago that the universe is at least twice the size they had previously believed. It has over 100 billion galaxies, which we believe He created and are held together by the word of His command (Hebrews 1).
>
> He, this same great Creator God, died for our sins, was raised from the dead and now lives within us in all of His mighty power, love, and wisdom. The Great Commission is His idea!

Therefore, we cannot ask Him for too much in laborers, money, technology, and other resources if they are to help fulfill His Great Commission. This is provided our hearts and motives are pure and we do what we do for His glory and praise.

By God's grace and the enabling of the Holy Spirit, the next two years will be the most exciting and spiritually fruitful for all of history…Let us commit ourselves to pray for one another and for the resources…necessary to finish the task.[3]

Christ alone can build a great church. He will first use you and others to build a *praying church* that accesses endless resources from our amazing God. When He has built that church, let us not forget the One who did the building. Do not let the growth of ministries in the church displace the supremacy of the Builder! Remember the parting words of Moses to Israel, after decades of learning prayer in the wilderness:

> It shall be, when the Lord your God brings you into the land of which He swore to your fathers…to give you large and beautiful cities which you did not build, houses full of all good things, which you did not fill, hewn-out wells which you did not dig, vineyards and olive trees which you did not plant—when you have eaten and are full—then beware, lest you forget the Lord who brought you out of the land of Egypt, from the house of bondage (Deuteronomy 6:10–12).

I encourage you to take time as soon as possible to work through the application that follows the Prayer Response and Personal Reflection below. This will help you begin targeting prayer concerns for your church. The steps will show you how to bring these concerns before your church leaders.

We have come a long way in our exploration of God's arena of prayer. In surveying God's universal position to our role in prayer, we have learned the mighty power of God which is right now conforming history to His eternal plan. We also discovered how to live and advance as a member of God's great prayer army. From our mountaintop position in God's theater of operations, we can take a final look at the possibilities before us in the arena of prayer.

Prayer Response

My Father, will You revive the people of our church? Please enlarge Your reviving work in me. Help me to remember that, with Your grace and the Holy Spirit's infilling, I can accomplish Your purposes. Build me into an instrument of prayer in our congregation. Fill me with Your vision for prayer that I may align all my activity with that vision. I ask this in the name of Jesus, amen.

Personal Reflection

- In what ways might you motivate people in your church to pray?
- If you are active in a prayer cell how could you enlarge it?
- How could a Prayer Escalade change how your church ministers?

Practical Step

Appendix F provides sample worksheets on which to compile a full menu of church prayer goals. There is one page each for your Acts 1:8 local, national, missionary, and frontier objectives. There is also a worksheet for a ministry other than a church.

For practice, fill out each of these samples. Following the "Operation 1: Targeting" information highlighted earlier in the chapter, identify these areas for your church. Use a blank sheet for the exercise. Then use the following instructions with your church.

1. Discuss the idea with, and get input from, your pastor or church decision-making body.

2. Specify details on the worksheet. List names, factors, and needs involved in your church goals.

3. To thoroughly cover each one, expand the categories as needed.

4. Subdivide the big targets into reasonably sized individual portions.

5. Set up your own finalized version of targeted church goals.

6. Share your sheet with your pastor for his approval.

7. Get together with a church prayer committee.

8. Work through the remaining three target-category worksheets.

Once you have adopted your church prayer goals, prayerfully consider holding a Prayer Escalade in your church.

CHAPTER 21

Seizing the
OPPORTUNITIES

Mount Everest in Central Asia is the tallest mountain in the world. In 1953, Sir Edmund Hillary and Tensing Norgay were the first men to scale its peak. At the time, I read about their reaction upon reaching the summit.

Hillary stood up to view the landscape, disregarding the danger of severe wind gusts. Norgay's shout of warning to Hillary is good for all spiritual mountain climbers: "To your knees, man! To your knees! It is too high to stand up here."

You reach your peak in God's prayer country and join with the Trinity in heavenly communion. You breathe His pure spiritual atmosphere. The scene is inspiring and the glory overwhelming. The privilege unspeakable.

You may be wondering how you can put into practice all you have learned about prayer. You may be asking yourself: *Where will I go from here? How will I use insights from these pages? What concepts will expand and enrich my personal life? Which ideas about prayer can I nurture among my friends? Am I able to move out in the prayer arena?*

To help you answer these concerns, I want to ask you one further question: Will you consider a *ministry* in prayer? The possibilities are many and urgent. It is very important now that you listen carefully to God. Do not dictate to Him, but ask for His leading and for confirmation from fellow believers. Then move out in obedience and faith to Him.

Keep in mind two perspectives: 1) your spiritual gift, and 2) your present position in life's journey. Start where you are and grow in your own prayer life. Learn to abide as a branch in Christ, your marvelous Vine. Follow Him through one open door after another.

You may have a calling to prayer. Pursue that calling. Start as an adoptive intercessor or plan a prayer journey for a target area on your heart. Watch for opportunities to serve as a prayer ambassador.

Are you a writer? Offer your services to your church or mission agency as a prayer news reporter and correspondent. Has God given you abilities in leadership? Accept invitations to lead or help a prayer group. Pray about serving, in His time, as a prayer group captain.

Are you involved in a prayer ministry? Open your thinking to expand your role and your field. Immense is the world yet to be possessed for our Lord Jesus. Is your gift in the area of administration? Explore the showers of opportunities for prayer coordinators or prayer correspondents. If your gift is teaching, contact a prayer ministry that has openings and training for instructors.

Has God given you the heart of a shepherd? Are you free to travel as a prayer missionary? Are you a counselor? The Christian world is opening more and more to persons with these valuable skills. Perhaps you are a minister of the gospel looking toward retirement years. You are a treasure to the family of God. The years ahead can be your most fruitful ones ever. Look for openings as a prayer pastor who serves in praying, teaching, speaking, leading, inspiring, writing, and encouraging. God may lead you in any or all of these.

Financial support may arise as an issue for some. Most prayer positions are not paid, but do not let finances deter a prayer calling. In His time, Christ can verify any call to you with a team of spiritual and financial partners.

Seek information from Christian organizations with growing prayer ministries. Start with your denominational or church-supported mission agency. Other agencies with information include:

- Great Commission Prayer Movement
  Campus Crusade for Christ
  100 Lake Hart Drive, Dept. 2800
  Orlando, FL 32832-0100
  (407) 826-2800

- Mission America
  5666 Lincoln Drive, Suite 100
  Edina, MN 55436
  (612) 912-0001

- The Navigators
  P.O. Box 6000
  Colorado Springs, CO 80934
  (719) 598-1212

- Operation Mobilization
  P.O. Box 444
  Tyrone, GA 30290-0444
  (770) 631-0432
  or write to their British address at:
  1 Sandileight Avenue
  Didsbury, Manchester
  M20 9LN United Kingdom

- Overseas Missionary Fellowship
  10 W. Dry Creek Circle
  Littleton, CO 80120
  (303) 730-4160
  International Headquarters
  2 Cluny Road
  Singapore, Singapore 1025

- World Prayer Center
  11005 Highway 83 North
  Colorado Springs, CO 80921
  (719) 262-9922

- Youth With A Mission International
  P.O. Box 26479
  Colorado Springs, CO 80936
  (719) 380-0505

I heard the late Senate Chaplain Richard C. Halverson speak at a National Day of Prayer banquet in Washington, D.C. He quoted Dr. Charles Steinmetz, an inventor and research scientist. "Some day, Christians are going to give themselves to a study of prayer; and when they do, it will change the world."

You are living in that day! Seize the hour. Invest your life in prayer. Take your place in God's plan. Help all the Christians you can to do the same. Work to win and disciple intercessors. Let worship be your life focus and yearn for your prayers to be the words you speak most often. Let your heavenly city loom high on your horizon. Let the arena of prayer be your home!

Pray for an explosion of the light of God into our darkened world. Your arena of prayer is big enough to accomplish it all!

Prayer Response

My holy Lord, Your truth highlights my accountability. I cannot bear to say "no" to You. Yet, I am timid about sustaining a life of prayer. One thing I can do is to offer my body to You as a living sacrifice, rather than by making promises. I offer myself to You now. Make me the kind of intercessor You want me to be.

I take in faith the assurance that Paul gave the Corinthians. Though he was writing about financial stewardship, his words are feeding my prayer stewardship: "God is able to make all grace abound toward you, that you, always having all sufficiency in all things, may have an abundance for every good work" (2 Corinthians 9:8).

You are giving me the privilege of a lifetime. Thank You for inviting me to live in Your presence. Lead me onward through Christ Jesus. Amen.

Personal Reflection

- How well have I prospered in my desire to pray?
- What steps have I failed to take or left incomplete?
- How can I move forward in prayer from my present level?

Practical Step

Write to one or more of the offices listed in this chapter and ask about opportunities for prayer ministry. Describe the type of work that is most on your heart. Ask for available learning and serving materials. Expect God to open the way for you into a growing ministry of prayer! God bless you!

PART FIVE

Resource Handbook for Fortifying YOUR PRAYER

The prayer that God particularly delights to answer is united prayer. There is power in the prayer of a single individual, and the prayer of individuals has wrought great things, but there is far greater power in united prayer.

R. A. Torrey, *The Power of Prayer*

Knowing God Personally

Just as there are physical laws that govern the physical universe, so are there spiritual laws that govern your relationship with God.

LAW 1: *God loves you and offers a wonderful plan for your life.*

God's Love
"God so loved the world that He gave His one and only Son, that whoever believes in Him shall not perish but have eternal life" (John 3:16, NIV).

God's Plan
[Christ speaking] "I came that they might have life, and might have it abundantly" [that it might be full and meaningful] (John 10:10).

Why is it that most people are not experiencing the abundant life? Because...

LAW 2: *Man is sinful and separated from God. Therefore, he cannot know and experience God's love and plan for his life.*

Man Is Sinful
"All have sinned and fall short of the glory of God" (Romans 3:23).

Man was created to have fellowship with God; but, because of his own stubborn self-will, he chose to go his own independent way and fellowship with God was broken. This self-will, characterized by an attitude of active rebellion or passive indifference, is an evidence of what the Bible calls sin.

Man Is Separated
"The wages of sin is death" [spiritual separation from God] (Romans 6:23).

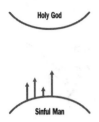

This diagram illustrates that God is holy and man is sinful. A great gulf separates the two. The arrows illustrate that man is continually trying to reach God and the abundant life through his own efforts, such as a good life, philosophy, or religion—but he inevitably fails.

The third law explains the only way to bridge this gulf...

LAW 3: *Jesus Christ is God's **only** provision for man's sin. Through Him you can know and experience God's love and plan for your life.*

He Died In Our Place
"God demonstrates His own love toward us, in that while we were yet sinners, Christ died for us" (Romans 5:8).

He Is the Only Way to God

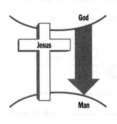

"Jesus said to him, 'I am the way, and the truth, and the life; no one comes to the Father but through Me'" (John 14:6).

This diagram illustrates that God has bridged the gulf that separates us from Him by sending His Son, Jesus Christ, to die on the cross in our place to pay the penalty for our sins.

It is not enough just to know these three laws...

LAW 4: *We must individually **receive** Jesus Christ as Savior and Lord; then we can know and experience God's love and plan for our lives.*

We Must Receive Christ
"As many as received Him, to them He gave the right to become children of God, even to those who believe in His name" (John 1:12).

We Receive Christ Through Faith
"By grace you have been saved through faith; and that not of yourselves, it is the gift of God; not as a result of works that no one should boast" (Ephesians 2:8,9).

When We Receive Christ, We Experience a New Birth
(Read John 3:1–8.)

We Receive Christ Through Personal Invitation
[Christ speaking] "Behold, I stand at the door and knock; if any one hears My voice and opens the door, I will come in to him" (Revelation 3:20).

Receiving Christ involves turning to God from self (repentance) and trusting Christ to come into our lives to forgive our sins and to make us what He wants us to be. Just to agree intellectually that Jesus Christ is the Son of God and that He died on the cross for our sins is not enough. Nor is it enough to have an emotional experience. We receive Jesus Christ by faith, as an act of the will.

These two circles represent two kinds of lives:

Self-Directed Life
S – Self is on the throne
† – Christ is outside the life
● – Interests are directed by self, often resulting in discord and frustration

Christ-Directed Life
† – Christ is in the life and on the throne
S – Self is yielding to Christ
● – Interests are directed by Christ, resulting in harmony with God's plan

Which circle best represents your life?

Which circle would you like to have represent your life?

The following explains how you can receive Christ:

You Can Receive Christ Right Now by Faith Through Prayer
(Prayer is talking with God)

God knows your heart and is not so concerned with your words as He is with the attitude of your heart. The following is a suggested prayer:

> *Lord Jesus, I need You. Thank You for dying on the cross for my sins. I open the door of my life and receive You as my Savior and Lord. Thank You for forgiving my sins and giving me eternal life. Take control of the throne of my life. Make me the kind of person You want me to be.*

Does this prayer express the desire of your heart? If it does, I invite you to pray this prayer right now, and Christ will come into your life, as He promised.

How to Know That Christ Is in Your Life

Did you receive Christ into your life? According to His promise in Revelation 3:20, where is Christ right now in relation to you? Christ said that He would come into your life. Would He mislead you? On what authority do you know that God has answered your prayer? (The trustworthiness of God Himself and His Word.)

The Bible Promises Eternal Life to All Who Receive Christ

"God has given us eternal life, and this life is in His Son. He who has the Son has the life; he who does not have the Son of God does not have the life" (1 John 5:11–13).

Thank God often that Christ is in your life and that He will never leave you (Hebrews 13:5). You can know on the basis of His promise that Christ lives in you and that you have eternal life from the very moment you invite Him in. He will not deceive you.

An important reminder...

Do Not Depend on Feelings

The promise of God's Word, the Bible—not our feelings—is our authority. The Christian lives by faith (trust) in the trustworthiness of God Himself and His Word. This train diagram illustrates the relationship among fact (God and His Word), faith (our trust in God and His Word), and feeling (the result of our faith and obedience). (Read John 14:21.)

 The train will run with or without the caboose. However, it would be useless to attempt to pull the train by the caboose. In the same way, as Christians we do not depend on feelings or emotions, but we place our faith (trust) in the trustworthiness of God and the promises of His Word.

Now That You Have Received Christ

The moment you received Christ by faith, as an act of the will, many things happened, including the following:

- Christ came into your life (Revelation 3:20; Colossians 1:27).
- Your sins were forgiven (Colossians 1:14).
- You became a child of God (John 1:12).
- You received eternal life (John 5:24).
- You began the great adventure for which God created you (John 10:10).

Can you think of anything more wonderful that could happen to you than receiving Christ? Would you like to thank God in prayer right now for what He has done for you? By thanking God, you demonstrate your faith.

To enjoy your new life to the fullest…

Suggestions for Christian Growth

Spiritual growth results from trusting Jesus Christ. A life of faith will enable you to trust God increasingly with every detail of your life, and to practice the following:

G   *Go* to God in prayer daily (John 15:7).

R   *Read* God's Word daily (Acts 17:11); begin with the Gospel of John.

O   *Obey* God moment by moment (John 14:21).

W   *Witness* for Christ by your life and words (Matthew 4:19; John 15:8).

T   *Trust* God for every detail of your life (1 Peter 5:7).

H   *Holy Spirit*—allow Him to control and empower your daily life and witness (Galatians 5:16,17; Acts 1:8; Ephesians 5:18).

Fellowship in a Good Church

God's Word instructs us not to forsake "the assembling of ourselves together" (Hebrews 10:25). If you do not belong to a church, do not wait to be invited. Take the initiative; call the pastor of a nearby church where Christ is honored and His Word is preached. Start this week, and make plans to attend regularly.

Attributes of God

The apostle John gives three comprehensive statements about God:

"God is life" (Spirit, breath).   John 4:24

"God is light."   1 John 1:5

"God is love."   1 John 4:8

All of God's attributes (qualities) can be arranged within these three aspects of His being. For spiritual adventure and growth, practice worshiping and praising Him for each quality of His nature. Use a Bible concordance to find Scriptures relating to each attribute.

God Is Life.

A Person	Eternal	Infinite	Our Creator
Self-existent	Omnipresent	Three-in-One	Provident
Changeless	Omniscient	Full of Glory	Heavenly
Perfect	Omnipotent	Good	Spirit

God Is Light.

Holy	Virtuous	Vengeful	Truth
Faithful	Our Savior	Righteous	Pure
Orderly	Just	Wrathful	Sovereign

God Is Love.

Merciful	Gracious	Patient	Forgiving
Our Father	The Son	Caring	Peace
Full of Grief	Tender	Joy	The Good Shepherd

Personal Prayer Plan Worksheets

One-Week Worksheet

Acts 1:8	Sun	Mon	Tue	Wed	Thu	Fri	Sat
My Jerusalem (local sphere)							
My Judea (state/nation)							
My Samaria (mission fields)							
My Frontiers (uttermost parts)							

Sample One-Week Prayer Plan

Acts 1:8	Sun	Mon	Tue	Wed	Thu	Fri	Sat
My Jerusalem (local sphere)	Church	Family	Personal ministry	Community	City	Personal needs	Personal goals
My Judea (state/nation)	County	State	Nation	Courts	Schools	Evangelistic movements	Churches
My Samaria (mission fields)	World	Africa	Asia	Europe	Latin America	Middle East	North America
My Frontiers (uttermost parts)	Unreached areas	Intercessors	Laborers	Receptivity	Evangelism	Discipling	Funding

215

Personal Prayer Plan
One-Month Worksheet

Acts 1:8	Sun	Mon	Tue	Wed	Thu	Fri	Sat
WEEK 1							
My Jerusalem (local sphere)							
My Judea (state/nation)							
My Samaria (mission fields)							
My Frontiers (uttermost parts)							
WEEK 2							
My Jerusalem (local sphere)							
My Judea (state/nation)							
My Samaria (mission fields)							
My Frontiers (uttermost parts)							
WEEK 3							
My Jerusalem (local sphere)							
My Judea (state/nation)							
My Samaria (mission fields)							
My Frontiers (uttermost parts)							
WEEK 4							
My Jerusalem (local sphere)							
My Judea (state/nation)							
My Samaria (mission fields)							
My Frontiers (uttermost parts)							

APPENDIX D

Interdenominational Prayer Meetings

By C. Peter Wagner,
AD2000 United Prayer Track Coordinator

T HE AD2000 MOVEMENT is an attempt to bring together the whole Body of Christ with a focus on evangelizing the world by the year 2000. A wide variety of Christian traditions is represented, and experience has shown that certain behavior patterns, especially in group or corporate prayer, are more appropriate for maintaining harmony than others.

As our overall track philosophy, we are using a statement developed by Every Home for Christ with the permission of Dick Eastman:

Remember that the moment two or more of us unite in prayer, we become a symphony. As such:

- We blend together in unity respecting the fact that we represent all of Christ's body.

- We realize that, like a symphony with its different instruments, there are a wide variety of traditions when it comes to prayer.

- We commit ourselves to accepting one another as we are, while disciplining ourselves to use wisdom and caution if we think anything we might do would offend a brother or sister.

We want all those who participate to be themselves. We must not quench the Spirit. There are no restrictions at all on prayer styles in prayer groups of like tradition. Yet some of these styles may not be appropriate in groups of mixed traditions.

Here are some of the specific areas in which wisdom, caution, spiritual discernment, and good manners need to be used:

Body Language

Body language is an important part of prayer. Raising hands, kneeling, and lying prostrate on the floor are not usually issues. Some pray with eyes closed and some with eyes open, some raise their chins, others lower their chins. Clapping, dancing, "falling in the Spirit," unrestrained laughter, and roaring are not as widely accepted, however, and special caution should be used by those accustomed to them. Blowing, hissing, and physically "travailing" should be avoided. At the same time, spiritual travail in prayer, at times with "groanings which cannot be uttered" (Romans 8:26) may be expected.

Prophecy

We encourage hearing from God and using the prophetic gifts. Prudence in communicating words from God in an interdenominational meeting will avoid such phrases as "thus saith the Lord" or using the first person for God. Prophecies can be prayed back to God: "God we hear you saying..." or expressed to the group with statements like "I think God may be saying to us..." and expecting others to agree if it is a true word.

In all cases, care must be taken that prophetic gifts are not publicly used apart from the covering, permission, and spiritual authority of the person designated to preside over the particular session. Prudence dictates that, particularly when the prophetic word has directional content (as opposed, for instance, to devotional content), explicit permission be sought from the presider before the word is given.

Tongues

It is no secret that the most sensitive issue is tongues. The AD2000 Movement seeks to balance 1 Corinthians 14:39, "Do not forbid to speak with tongues," with the next verse, "Let all things be done decently and in order" (1 Corinthians 14:40). In our interdenominational Prayer Track meetings we feel that individuals may use tongues in a whisper or even in a louder voice when all are praying aloud in a concert and no one person's voice stands out above the others. But we feel it is not prudent to use tongues when one is audibly leading the whole group in prayer. We also need to agree that we will not use messages from God in tongues with interpretation.

In Summary

Good will is an essential personal characteristic for all who participate. This is a day in which we are seeing a visible spiritual unity of the Body of Christ, which is unprecedented both in quantity and quality. We are bold enough to believe that it is an answer to Jesus' prayer "that they all may be one...that the world might believe" (John 17:21).

Synonyms for Prayer

Alphabetical List	Number of Occurrences in Bible	
Abide	Pray, prayer	511
Access	Speak	484
Adore, adoration	Come to Me	232
Answer God	Praise	216
Ask	Say to the Lord	192
Call	Cry, cried to the Lord	168
Come	Hear, heard the Lord	158
Cry, cried to the Lord	Thanksgiving, giving thanks	109
Delight in God	Presence (in Thy)	108
Fellowship with God	Fight (spiritual)	103
Fight (spiritual)	Worship	102
Hear, heard the Lord	Seek the Lord	81
Intercede, intercession	Abide in Me	77
Intreat	Supplication	57
Knock	Delight in the Lord	50
Look to Me	Walk with God	50
Meet the Lord	Plead	35
Minister to the Lord	Call	34
Plead	Wait on/for the Lord	26
Praise	Meet/met the Lord	23
Pray, prayer	Intreat	22
Presence (in Thy)	Answer God	18
Say to the Lord	Ask	11
Seek	Adore, adoration	11

Alphabetical List	**Number of Occurrences in Bible**	
Speak	Intercede	11
Supplication	Knock	4
Take hold of my strength	Fellowship with God	3
Talk with God	Talk with God	3
Thanksgiving, giving thanks	Access	2
Wait on/for the Lord	Look to God	1
Walk with God	Minister to the Lord	1
Worship	Take hold of My strength	1
Wrestle	Wrestle	1

Prayer Adoption Register

(Adapt this chart for your church's local prayer concerns. Match your church groups with prayer needs related to their area of ministry. For example, the children's department may want to pray for the elementary school and the youth group for local junior and senior high schools.)

Our Jerusalem

City and Neighborhood Boundaries _____

Prayer Targets	Group Responsible	Prayer Volunteers
Church Area:		
Community A	_____	_____
Community B	_____	_____
School A	_____	_____
School B	_____	_____
Sectors of Society:		
Mayor	_____	_____
City Council	_____	_____
Police/fire depts.	_____	_____
Fellow Church Members:		
The elderly	_____	_____
Church families	_____	_____
Non-Christian parents and spouses	_____	_____
Those who are ill	_____	_____

Our Judea

(Adapt this chart for your church's prayer concerns. Include the names of government leaders so volunteers can pray for them by name.)

Nation _____ State _____ County _____

Prayer Targets	Group Responsible	Prayer Volunteers
Nation:		
Executive Branch:		
President, Vice Pres.	_____	_____
Cabinet	_____	_____
Legislative Branch:		
Senators	_____	_____
Representatives	_____	_____
Judicial Branch:		
Supreme Court	_____	_____
State:		
Governor, Lt. Gov.	_____	_____
Cabinet	_____	_____
State legislators	_____	_____
County:		
Board of Supervisors	_____	_____
Department chiefs	_____	_____
School district officials and personnel	_____	_____

Our Samaria

(Duplicate the following chart for each missionary your church supports.)

Our Missionaries and Their Fields

Missionary: _____

Prayer Targets   **Prayer Volunteers**

Mission goals   _____

Opposing forces   _____

Waiting frontiers   _____

Field needs   _____

Personal needs   _____

Our Frontier

(Adapt the following categories to your church's adopted area.)

The Unreached Area Adopted by Our Church _____

Prayer Targets	Group Responsible	Prayer Volunteers
Mission field needs:		
Spiritual Readiness	_____	_____
Translations (literature, Bible)	_____	_____
Radio broadcasts	_____	_____
Government favor	_____	_____
Freedom to preach the gospel	_____	_____
Laborers	_____	_____
The harvest	_____	_____
Personnel:		
Pioneer evangelists	_____	_____
More intercessors	_____	_____
Disciples	_____	_____
Home groups	_____	_____
National pastors	_____	_____
Health and safety	_____	_____
Supplies:		
Housing	_____	_____
Finances	_____	_____
Vehicles	_____	_____
Materials, films	_____	_____
Equipment	_____	_____

Ministry or Other Christian Organization
Prayer Adoption Register

(Adapt this worksheet to the prayer needs of your ministry. Make a copy for each person on your prayer team.)

Ministry _____ Director _____

Prayer Coordinator _____ Time Period _____

Department Targets   **Adoptive Intercessors**
Ministry Goals

_____   _____
_____   _____
_____   _____
_____   _____

Personnel
   Staff

_____   _____
_____   _____
   Internal intercessors   _____
   External intercessors   _____
Finances

_____   _____
_____   _____

Materials/Equipment

_____   _____
_____   _____

Other

_____   _____
_____   _____

National Targets

_____   _____
_____   _____
_____   _____

World Targets   **Adoptive Intercessors**

_____   _____

_____   _____

_____   _____

Summary of Prayer Positions

Intercessor
Luke 2:36–38. A volunteer who seeks to 1) grow in prayer as a way of life, and 2) pray as the Lord leads, without requiring structural accountability.

Adoptive Intercessor
Romans 15:25–33. A person who accepts prayer responsibility for one or more ministries or target areas in the Great Commission of our Lord Jesus Christ.

Discipler
Philippians 4:9. An intercessor who shares scriptural prayer principles from his or her own life with a faithful, teachable learner.

Prayer Ambassador
Romans 1:8–12. An intercessor who travels to the scene of a special Great Commission advance and ministers short-term, usually at his or her own expense. He or she intercedes for this special endeavor and disciples local intercessors.

Writer/Correspondent
1 John 2:12–14. Intercessors with the gift of communicating spiritual concepts in written form.

Corporate Volunteers

Group Leader
Acts 16:13–15. An intercessor who accepts an appointment to start and/or lead neighbors or colleagues in prayer for Great Commission goals.

Captain
2 Timothy 2:2. An intercessor with administrative ability to assist leaders of two or more prayer groups in:
- Recruiting and training new leaders
- Forming new prayer groups
- Supplying prayer materials

Coordinator
Acts 18:23. A leader who spreads a prayer movement in a church, city, culture, campus, country, or continent.

Representative
Colossians 4:7–9. An intercessor trained to appear at public events in behalf of an agency, usually in his or her larger residential area. The representative is able to provide prayer information, materials, encouragement, and assistance to area ministers and leaders.

Editor
Hebrews 13:22. An intercessor with the ability to sort, sift, condense, communicate, and publish material available in today's increasingly voluminous sources of information.

Instructor/Trainer
Ephesians 4:12. An intercessor with the ability to teach prayer in classes, conferences, retreats, schools of prayer, workshops, and leadership training classes.

Helper
Galatians 5:13. An intercessor with the gift of serving and helping others generate effective prayer.

Staff Personnel

Funding is an important consideration for the following positions. Financial arrangements for a position depend upon 1) the requirements involved, 2) the available corporate monetary resources, and 3) the individual resources available to the ministering person.

Ministering persons may consider themselves as missionaries and enlist supporting partners in line with the policies of their agency. Parent bodies who benefit from their intercessors should make growing budgetary provisions for developing prayer ministries.

All prayer ministries need to be authorized by a church or agency, according to the doctrinal, administrative, financial, and procedural regulations of that body.

Missionary
Daniel 9,10. An intercessor who makes a long-term move to another location and serves a prayer ministry there. John "Praying" Hyde is an example.

Pastor/Minister
1 Timothy 2:1–10. An intercessor who is ordained to the Christian ministry and is called by a church or agency to lead prayer development within that body of Christian believers.

Administrator
Ephesians 6:10–18. An intercessor who can help a prayer team to identify and grasp organizational objectives.

Prayer Correspondent Job Description

ERNIE PYLE WAS A World War II hero. He carried no gun; stormed no hill. As a War Correspondent, Pyle represented a courageous corps of people who helped keep a nation united in a critical cause. He roved battlefronts, often under fire, and did a terrific job. He was killed in action.

The Great Commission of Jesus Christ can be advanced immeasurably by people who fill a similar role in God's spiritual war. Call them Prayer Correspondents. Their task is to unite the Body of Christ in spiritual warfare.

Purpose:
To provide information to intercessors and to enlist and train others for the same kind of service

Qualifications:
- A commitment to fulfillment of the Great Commission in Christ
- An awareness of the spiritual conflict involved in world evangelization
- A hope-filled attitude that can both inspire and challenge Christian workers
- A desire to nurture Great Commission prayer
- The ability to follow an organization's communication policies in a prioritized, accurate, and concise manner

Responsibilities:

- Communicate a flow of Great Commission information between mission fields and intercessors.
- Develop a model personal prayer ministry.
- Recruit and train other Correspondents on domestic and foreign mission fields.
- Provide a communications center to assist with and develop a visualization of global prayer.

Recruiting Procedures:

Ministry leaders who want to acquire a Prayer Correspondent may find the following preparation steps helpful. Success in recruiting and retaining such persons is dependent on the Correspondent's access to objectives, plans, structure, and progress of the organizational body.

1. Acquaint the Correspondent with your Vision (Matthew 9:36–38).

2. Expose him or her to *priority* issues and objectives (John 15:15,16).

3. Help him or her to enlist other strategic Correspondents (1 Peter 2:9).

4. Provide operational facilities (note availability of facilities in Luke 2:36–38).

Prayer Coordinator Job Description

Purpose:
To develop a prayer-leadership team for the Great Commission objectives of the church

Qualifications:
- A steadfast, growing prayer life
- Ability to lead leaders
- Agreement with doctrinal position and administrative policies of the church
- Commitment to revival and fulfillment of the Great Commission of Jesus Christ

Responsibilities:
- Model, encourage, and nurture various forms of prayer
- Serve as a channel of communication between church staff and congregational prayer units
- Stimulate, assist, and coordinate prayer activities

Duties:
- Intercede.
- See that a prayer leader is elected or appointed for each division of the body.

- Meet with prayer leaders periodically to encourage, evaluate, and refine the prayer ministry.
- Promote the Great Commission prayer goals of the body.
- Train a growing team of prayer leaders.
- Plan prayer studies, workshops, classes, seminars, and conferences for recommendation to decision-makers.
- Establish and maintain a spiritual war room to monitor progress.
- Help leaders in each division to use prayer agendas.
- Assist church staff in planning an annual prayer conference.
- Confer with church staff and prayer leaders concerning big prayer issues.

Accountable to:
- The pastor or ministry leader
- The organizational network of prayer leaders

Term of service set by the official body in its volunteer and staff policies.

A Spiritual War Room

Rationale:
National governments maintain military war rooms to display all kinds of scenarios for strategic planning. Churches need a similar facility for their world role.

Scripture Precedent:
- Gilgal (Joshua 4:19; 9:6; 10:6,43): Base camp for the Promised Land
- Hezekiah and Isaiah (Isaiah 37:14–38): House of the Lord
- Apostles (Acts 6:1–8): Guidance for the early Church
- Antioch (Acts 13:1–4): Launching of the missionary movement
- Corinth (Romans 15:17–33): Overview of Paul's ministry

Purposes:
- Planning prayer strategies, including ministry objectives, mobilization, policy, and progress tracking
- Providing guidance for leadership interaction, intercession, and action
- Assessing "what the Holy Spirit is saying to the churches"
- Keeping intercessors informed of developing data
- Training staff, trainers, coordinators, and intercessors

- Preparing and stocking materials
- Identifying spiritual targets
- Mapping territory for spiritual responsibility
- Visualizing progress for praise or prayer
- Reporting on answers to prayer

Required Items:
- A room or area set apart for visualizing church prayer action
- Maps of entire areas to be served by the church
- Charts depicting objectives, progress, problems, and praise items
- List of volunteers and their adopted prayer targets

Activities:
- Periodic strategy meetings
- Intercessory prayer meetings
- Research
- Data tabulation
- Visualization using graphs, maps, and charts
- Communication center
- Personnel enlistment and deployment

Pastor's Prayer Support Team

T HE PASTOR'S PRAYER Support Team is designed to provide the pastor (or ministry director) with a block of prayer that can be used to launch all activities of the church, including movements of evangelism and discipleship.

Ideally, the pastor selects 31 men, each of whom will join him as a prayer partner for a specific day each month. If 31 men aren't available, then the pastor will begin with the number of available men. In this case, some men will pray more than one day per month. For example, if only seven men could be enlisted initially, they would be involved one day each week for the entire month.

One pastor keeps a list of his praying men near his telephone, listing both business and residential telephone numbers. He calls each man one or two days before his prayer commitment as a reminder and to discuss prayer needs. Other pastors meet their men weekly to hear results and to share new challenges to pray. Urgent requests can be sent to all the men simultaneously via E-mail, fax, or pager.

On each Sunday morning, the seven men who have been praying the previous seven days meet to pray during the worship service(s).

The pastor's wife could implement the same strategy, inviting the women to meet during the Sunday school hour to pray for the teachers.

This plan provides the pastor (or ministry director) and his wife with continuous prayer support throughout the entire year, producing the power base for the entire ministry.

Many other situations could be applied to this plan as you allow the Holy Spirit to develop creative ideas in your prayer ministry. Remember that "the effective prayer of a righteous man can accomplish much" (James 5:16).

Church Prayer Escalade Worksheets

My Prayer Escalade

(Use this form as an example to remind volunteers of their prayer commitment.)

DATES: _____ to _____

"The weapons of our warfare are not of the flesh, but divinely powerful for the destruction of fortresses."—2 Corinthians 10:4 (NASB)

I AM A VOLUNTEER IN GOD'S SPIRITUAL CONQUEST. I WILL SEEK TO PRAY DAILY, AS HE LEADS ME,

FOR _____
(Church Prayer Target)

AND FOR _____
(Beyond Our Church)

"Call to Me, and I will answer you, and show you great and mighty things, which you do not know." —Jeremiah 33:3

Church Prayer Escalade

Target	Volunteer

CHURCH ACTIVITIES

Worship Services _____

Ministry Training _____

Care Circles _____

Church Families _____

Members' Neighborhoods _____

Church Events _____

LEADERS

Pastor and Family _____

Staff/Personnel and Families _____

Elders and Families _____

Deacons and Families _____

Deaconesses and Families _____

Ushers/Greeters _____

Property Care _____

MINISTRY AREAS

Christian Education _____

Nursery _____

Children's Ministries _____

Youth Ministries _____

Women's Ministries _____

Men's Ministries _____

WIDER-AREA CONCERNS

City _____

County _____

State _____

Country _____

MISSIONS *(list missionaries and fields)*

_____   _____

_____   _____

_____   _____

_____   _____

End Notes

Chapter 1: Prayer and Our Endangered World

1. This account is attributed to Jonathan Chao and his staff at the Chinese Christian Center for World Evangelization in Hong Kong.
2. Campus Crusade for Christ, "East Asia Report," 1997.

Chapter 2: Encountering the Supernatural

1. Dr. and Mrs. Ralph Winter founded this Center in 1978.
2. Bill and Vonette Bright founded Campus Crusade for Christ International in 1951 in Brentwood, California. The ministry has grown to include more than fifty ministries, of which university campuses are still a major emphasis. As of 1999, the movement enlists more than 14,000 full-time missionary staff and 300,000 associate and volunteer staff in 172 countries.
3. The AD2000 and Beyond Movement is a coalition of mission agencies that have Great Commission completion plans under way for the year 2000. Tremendous progress in world evangelization occurred during its 10-year tenure. By prior agreement, the AD2000 coalition concludes its work in 2000 and passes its leadership on to other evangelical world networks.
4. PrayUSA!, based in Houston, Texas, grew out of the United Prayer Track of the AD2000 Movement. It sponsors forty days of prayer and fasting for the U.S., drawing up to 15 million people to pray.
5. Patrick Johnstone, *Operation World* (Grand Rapids, MI: Zondervan Publishing House, 1993), 31.
6. One of the most complete listings of prayer ministries is available from Global Harvest Ministries, P.O. Box 63060, Colorado Springs, CO 80962-3060; (719) 262-9922.

Chapter 3: God's Theater of Operations

1. St. Augustine, Bishop of Hippo, *Confessions of St. Augustine (354–430 A.D.), An Early Church Father* (Westwood, NJ: The Christian Library, 1984).
2. This is my translation of these verses from the Greek language in which the New Testament was written.
3. S. D. Gordon, *Quiet Talks on Prayer* (Westwood, NJ: The Christian Library, 1984).

4. Quoted in Kenneth W. Osbeck, *Amazing Grace* (Grand Rapids, MI: Kruegel Publications, 1990).

Chapter 6: Our Prayers and God's Sovereignty
1. Bishop Wellington Boone, address to the Fourth Fasting and Prayer Conference in Dallas, Texas, November 1997.

Chapter 7: Prayer and God the Father
1. Robert Foster, "The Challenge," a personal newsletter, November 1, 1984.

Chapter 8: My Role in God's Arena
1. Quoted in Kathy Collord Miller, ed., *God's Abundance: 365 Days to a Simple Life* (Lancaster, PA: Starbust, Publisher, 1997), June 25.
2. For current information on the progress of world evangelization, contact: Global Harvest Ministries, P.O. Box 63060, Colorado Springs, CO 80962-6030.

Chapter 9: My Coach, the Holy Spirit
1. Robert Foster, *The Challenge*, personal newsletter, November 1, 1984.
2. J. P. Lange, *Commentary on the Holy Scriptures*, vol. 10 (Grand Rapids, MI: Zondervan Publishing House, 1960), 276,277.
3. *Intercessors for America* newsletter (Leesburg, VA: Intercessors for America, October 4, 1997), vol. 24, #11.

Chapter 10: Jesus, My Connection in Heaven
1. Andrew Murray, *Holiest of All* (Springdale, PA: Whitaker House, 1996).
2. S. D. Gordon, *Quiet Talks on Prayer* (Westwood, NJ: The Christian Library, 1984).

Chapter 11: Meeting God Face to Face
1. St. Augustine, Bishop of Hippo, *Confessions of St. Augustine (354–430 A.D.), An Early Church Father* (Westwood, NJ: The Christian Library, 1984).

Chapter 12: A Heart That God Will Hear
1. For a more detailed explanation of God's holiness, see Bill Bright, *God: Discover His Character* (Orlando, FL: NewLife Publications, 1999) or Stephen Charnock, *The Existence and Attributes of God*, vol. 2 (Grand Rapids, MI: Baker Books, 1996), 108–208.

Chapter 13: Growing in Faith
1. Dawson Trotman, *Born to Reproduce* (Colorado Springs, CO: NavPress, 1975.

Chapter 14: Winning Battles
1. Story taken from Paul Eshleman, *The Touch of Jesus* (Orlando, FL: NewLife Publications, 1995), 15–21.
2. Eshleman, 16.

3. Eshleman, 18.

Chapter 15: Exploring My Celestial Home

1. Jim Elliott, edited by Elisabeth Elliot, *The Journals of Jim Elliott* (Old Tappan, NJ: Fleming H. Revell Co., 1978).

Chapter 16: Becoming Part of a Prayer Movement

1. Ralph Winter, excerpted from his missions-changing address, "The Hidden Peoples," Lausanne Congress on World Evangelism, 1974. Copies of the address are available through William Carey Library, Pasadena, California.
2. Todd Johnson, "The Crisis of Missions: The Historical Development of the Idea of the Evangelization of the World by the Year 1900," *Mission Frontiers* (Pasadena, CA: U.S. Center for World Mission, August 1988).
3. "Praying Through the Window," an international month of prayer has enlisted up to 50 million praying people every two years.
4. Daniel 6:10 is a key verse in the life of this great prophet. See chapters 9 and 10 for illustrations of Daniel's passion in prayer.
5. Bill Bright, "Is It Still Possible to Change the World?" brochure (Orlando, FL: Campus Crusade for Christ International).
6. C. Peter Wagner, *Confronting the Powers* (Ventura, CA: Regal Books, 1996), 11.
7. S. D. Gordon, *Quiet Talks on Prayer* (Westwood, N.J.: The Christian Library, 1984).
8. David Bryant, *In the Gap: What It Means to Be a World Christian* (Ventura, CA: Regal Books, 1984).
9. Porter Barrington, compiler, *The Christian Life New Testament, Master Outlines and Notes, New King James Version* (Nashville, TN: Thomas Nelson, Inc., 1969) 12.

Chapter 17: Feasting and Fasting

1. For more information about the growing fasting movement, see Bill Bright's book, *The Coming Revival* (Orlando, FL: *NewLife* Publications, 1995).
2. *Nelson's Illustrated Bible Dictionary* (Nashville, TN: Thomas Nelson Publishers, 1986) 379.

Chapter 18: Developing Prayer Strategies

1. Pastor Thorlief Holmglad, in a presentation at a Prayer Fellowship conference, Pacific Palisades, California, in the late 1950s.
2. Patrick Johnstone, *Operation World* (Grand Rapids, MI: Zondervan Publishing House, 1993), 11.

Chapter 19: Recruiting Prayer Warriors

1. *Operation World* is available through Zondervan Publishing House, Grand Rapids, Michigan.

2. Five Bible study courses on prayer are recommended and available from the Great Commission Prayer Movement, 100 Lake Hart Drive, Dept. 2800, Orlando, Florida, 32832-0100. All are complete with both student and instructor guides. They include:

Change Your World Through Prayer and Fasting
Building a Strategic Prayer Movement
Understanding Prayer
The King and the Dragon (spiritual warfare)
Birthing Spiritual Movements

3. For more information, contact The Macedonian Project at 100 Lake Hart Drive, Dept. 4000, Orlando, Florida 32832-0100, or call (407) 826-2810.

4. Jim Cymbala, *Fresh Wind, Fresh Fire* (Grand Rapids, MI: Zondervan Publishing House, 1997), 150.

5. Armin Gesswein, revivalist, evangelist, and founder/director of Revival Prayer Fellowship, San Juan Capistrano, California, made this statement on numerous public occasions.

Chapter 20: Building a Praying Church

1. To read the story of this prayer miracle, see Jim Cymbala, *Fresh Wind, Fresh Fire* (Grand Rapids, MI: Zondervan Publishing House, 1997).

2. Jack Hayford, *Glory on Your House* (Tarrytown, NJ: Chosen Books, Fleming H. Revell, 1995), 238–251.

3. From a letter to the Campus Crusade for Christ International staff, December 23, 1998.

Bibliography

Balsiger, David W., Whims, Joette, and Hunskor, Melody. *The Incredible Power of Prayer* (Wheaton, IL: Tyndale House Publishers, Inc., 1998).

Baughen, Michael. *Breaking the Prayer Barrier* (Wheaton, IL: Harold Shaw Publishers, 1981).

Billheimer, Paul. *Destined for the Throne* (Houston, TX: Christian Literature Crusade, 1975).

Bisagno, John. *The Power of Positive Prayer* (Grand Rapids, MI: Zondervan Publishing House, 1965).

Bright, Bill. *How to Pray With Confidence* (Orlando, FL: *NewLife* Publications, 1981).

Bright, Bill. *The Coming Revival* (Orlando, FL: *NewLife* Publications, 1995).

Bright, Vonette and Jennings, Ben. *Unleashing the Power of Prayer* (Chicago: Moody Press, 1986).

Bryant, David. *Concerts of Prayer* (Ventura, CA: Regal Books, 1988).

Bryant, David. *Messengers of Hope* (Grand Rapids, MI: Baker Book House, 1997).

Bush, Luis and Pugues, Beverly. *The Move of the Holy Spirit in the 10/40 Window* (Seattle, WA: YWAM Publishing, 1999).

Chadwick, Samuel. *God Listens* (Carol Stream, IL: Good News Publishers, 1973).

Christenson, Evelyn. *A Journey into Prayer* (Colorado Springs, CO: Chariot Victor Publishing, 1995).

Coleman, Robert. *Dry Bones Can Live Again* (Grand Rapids, MI: Fleming H. Revell Co., 1969).

Cymbala, Jim. *Fresh Wind, Fresh Fire* (Grand Rapids, MI: Zondervan Publishing House, 1997).

Duewel, Wesley. *Mighty Prevailing Prayer* (Grand Rapids, MI: Zondervan Publishing House, 1990).

Duewel, Wesley. *Touch the World Through Prayer* (Grand Rapids, MI: Zondervan Publishing House, 1986).

Finney, Charles Parkhurst. *Principles of Prayer* (Minneapolis: Bethany House, 1980).

Finney, Chris. *Prevailing Prayer* (Grand Rapids, MI: Kregel Publications, 1965).

Floyd, Ronnie. *The Power of Prayer and Fasting* (Nashville: Broadman and Holman Publishers, 1997).

Foster, Richard. *Prayer: Finding the Heart's True Home* (New York: HarperCollins Publishers, 1992).

Gesswein, Armin. *With One Accord in One Place* (Harrisburg, PA: Christian Publications, 1978).

Hawthorne, Kendrick. *Prayer Walking* (Lake Mary, FL: Creation House, 1993).

Hayford, Jack. *Prayer Is Invading the Impossible* (Plainfield, NJ: Logos International, 1977).

Henry, Matthew. *The Secret of Communion* (Grand Rapids, MI: Kregel Communications, 1991).

Hunter, W. Bingham. *The God Who Hears* (Downers Grove, FL: Intervarsity Press, 1986).

The Kneeling Christian (Grand Rapids, MI: Zondervan Publishing House, 1987).

MacArthur, John. *Jesus' Pattern of Prayer* (Chicago: Moody Press, 1981).

Matthews, Arthur. *Born for Battle* (Robesonia, PA: OMF Books, 1978).

Miller, Basil. *George Muller* (Wheaton, IL: Harold Shaw, 1981).

Mitchell, Curtis. *Praying Jesus' Way* (Grand Rapids, MI: Fleming H. Revell Co., 1977).

Moody, D. L. *Prevailing Prayer* (Chicago: Moody Press, 1981).

Murray, Andrew. *The Ministry of Intercessory Prayer* (Houston, TX: Christian Literature Crusade, 1983).

Murray, Andrew. *State of the Church* (Houston, TX: Christian Literature Crusade, 1983).

Murray, Andrew. *With Christ in the School of Prayer* (Houston, TX: Christian Literature Crusade, 1983).

Myers, Warren and Ruth. *Pray: How to Be Effective in Prayer* (Colorado Springs, CO: Navpress, 1983).

Nee, Watchman. *The Prayer Ministry of the Church* (New York: Christian Fellowship Publishers, 1973).

Ogilvie, Lloyd. *Praying with Power* (Ventura, CA: Regal Books, 1983).

Pink, Arthur. *A Guide to Fervent Prayer* (Grand Rapids, MI: Baker Book House, 1981).

Ravenlid, Leonard. *Revival Praying* (Minneapolis: Bethany House Publishers, 1962).

Rinker, Rosalind. *Communicating Love Through Prayer* (Grand Rapids, MI: Zondervan Publishing House, 1966).

Rinker, Rosalind. *Prayer, Conversing with God* (Grand Rapids, MI: Zondervan Publishing House, 1959).

Sanders, Oswald. *Prayer Power Unlimited* (Chicago: Moody Press, 1977).

Sorensen, Susan and Whims, Joette. *Kids P.R.A.Y.: An Elementary Teachers Guide to Adopt-A-Leader and the National Day of Prayer* (Colorado Springs, CO: National Day of Pray Task Force, 1999).

Sorensen, Susan and Whims, Joette. *Kit Cat's Time-Travel Adventure: The Story of the National Day of Prayer* (San Juan Capistrano, CA: Joy Publishing, 1999).

Taylor, Jack. *The Hallelujah Factor* (Nashville: Broadman Press, 1983).

Torrey, R. A. *The Power of Prayer* (Grand Rapids, MI: Zondervan Publishing House, 1924).

Wagner, Peter. *Breaking Strongholds in Your City* (Ventura, CA: Regal Books, 1993).

Wagner, Peter. *Confronting the Powers* (Ventura, CA: Regal Books, 1996).

Wiersbe, Warren. *Classic Sermons on Prayer* (Grand Rapids, MI: Kregel Publications, 1965).

Wiersbe, Warren. *Something Happens When Churches Pray* (Lincoln, NE: Back to the Bible, 1984).

Resources

Other Resources by Bill Bright

Resources for Fasting and Prayer

The Coming Revival: America's Call to Fast, Pray, and "Seek God's Face." This inspiring yet honest book explains how the power of fasting and prayer by millions of God's people can usher in a mighty spiritual revival and lift His judgment on America. *The Coming Revival* can equip Christians, their churches, and our nation for the greatest spiritual awakening since the first century.

7 Basic Steps to Successful Fasting and Prayer. This handy booklet gives practical steps to undertaking and completing a fast, suggests a plan for prayer, and offers an easy-to-follow daily nutritional schedule.

Preparing for the Coming Revival: How to Lead a Successful Fasting and Prayer Gathering. This easy-to-use handbook presents step-by-step instructions on how to plan and conduct a fasting and prayer gathering in your church or community. The book also contains creative ideas for teaching group prayer and can be used for a small group or large gatherings.

The Transforming Power of Fasting and Prayer. This follow-up book to *The Coming Revival* includes stirring accounts of Christians who have participated in the fasting and prayer movement that is erupting across the country.

Five Steps to Fasting and Prayer. The need for Christians who can lead our nation out of its moral morass is desperate. Fasting and prayer can be the answer for those who desire a deeper walk with God—and to influence our society for Christ. This five-part study teaches you how to tap into the power of fasting and prayer.

Resources for Group and Individual Study

Five Steps of Christian Growth. This five-lesson Bible study will help group members be sure that they are a Christian, learn what it means to grow as a Christian, experience the joy of God's love and forgiveness, and discover how to be filled with the Holy Spirit. Leader's and Study Guides are available.

Five Steps to Sharing Your Faith. This Bible study is designed to help Christians develop a lifestyle of introducing others to Jesus Christ. With these step-by-step lessons, believers can learn how to share their faith with confidence through the power of the Holy Spirit. Leader's and Study Guides are available.

Five Steps to Knowing God's Will. This five-week Bible study includes detailed information on applying the Sound Mind Principle to discover God's will. Both new and more mature Christians will find clear instructions useful for every aspect of decision-making. Leader's and Study Guides are available.

Five Steps to Making Disciples. This effective Bible study can be used for one-on-one discipleship, leadership evangelism training in your church, or a neighborhood Bible study group. Participants will learn how to begin a Bible study to disciple new believers as well as more mature Christians. Leader's and Study Guides are available.

Ten Basic Steps Toward Christian Maturity. These time-tested Bible studies offer a simple way to understand the basics of the Christian faith and provide believers with a solid foundation for growth. The product of many years of extensive development, the studies have been used by thousands. Leader's and Study Guides are available.

Introduction: The Uniqueness of Jesus

Step 1: The Christian Adventure

Step 2: The Christian and the Abundant Life

Step 3: The Christian and the Holy Spirit

Step 4: The Christian and Prayer

Step 5: The Christian and the Bible

Step 6: The Christian and Obedience

Step 7: The Christian and Witnessing

Step 8: The Christian and Giving

Step 9: Exploring the Old Testament
Step 10: Exploring the New Testament

A Handbook for Christian Maturity. This book combines the *Ten Basic Steps* Study Guides in one handy volume. The lessons can be used for daily devotions or with groups of all sizes.

Ten Basic Steps Leader's Guide. This book contains teacher's helps for the entire *Ten Basic Steps* Bible Study series. The lessons include opening and closing prayers, objectives, discussion starters, and suggested answers to the questions.

Resources for Christian Growth

Transferable Concepts. This series of time-tested messages teaches the principles of abundant Christian life and ministry. These "back-to-the-basics" resources help Christians grow toward greater spiritual maturity and fulfillment and live victorious Christian lives. These messages, available in book format and on video or audio cassette, include:

How You Can Be Sure You Are a Christian
How You Can Experience God's Love and Forgiveness
How You Can Be Filled With the Spirit
How You Can Walk in the Spirit
How You Can Be a Fruitful Witness
How You Can Introduce Others to Christ
How You Can Help Fulfill the Great Commission
How You Can Love By Faith
How You Can Pray With Confidence
How You Can Experience the Adventure of Giving
How You Can Study the Bible Effectively

A Man Without Equal. This book explores the unique birth, life, teachings, death, and resurrection of Jesus Christ and shows how He continues to change the way we live and think today. Available in book and video formats.

Life Without Equal. This inspiring book shows how Christians can experience pardon, purpose, peace, and power for living the Christian life. The book also explains how to release Christ's resurrection power to help change the world.

Have You Made the Wonderful Discovery of the Spirit-Filled Life? This booklet shows how you can discover the reality of the Spirit-filled life and live in moment-by-moment dependence on God.

The Holy Spirit: Key to Supernatural Living. This booklet helps you enter into the Spirit-filled life and explains how you can experience power and victory.

Promises: A Daily Guide to Supernatural Living. These 365 devotionals will help you remain focused on God's great love and faithfulness by reading and meditating on His promises each day. You will find your faith growing as you get to know our God and Savior better.

GOD: Discover His Character. Everything about our lives is determined and influenced by our view of God. Through these pages Dr. Bright will equip you with the biblical truths that will energize your walk with God. So when you're confused, you can experience His truth. When you're frightened, you can know His peace. When you're sad, you can live in His joy.

GOD: Discover His Character Video Series. In these 13 sessions, Dr. Bright's clear teaching is illustrated by fascinating dramas that bring home the truth of God's attributes in everyday life. This video series, with the accompanying leader's guide, is ideal for youth, college, and adult Sunday school classes or study groups.

> **Our Great Creator (Vol. I).** Dr. Bright explores God as all-powerful, ever-present, all-knowing, and sovereign—and how those attributes can give you hope and courage in life.

> **Our Perfect Judge (Vol. II).** God your perfect Judge, is holy, true, righteous, and just, and Dr. Bright explains how those characteristics help you to live a righteous life.

> **Our Gracious Savior (Vol. III).** Dr. Bright introduces you to the God who is loving, merciful, faithful, and unchangeable, and shows how you can experience those awesome attributes every day.

Response Form

☐ I have received Jesus Christ as my Savior and Lord as a result of reading this book.

☐ As a new Christian I want to know Christ better and experience the abundant Christian life.

☐ With God's help I will faithfully pray for revival, the harvest, laborers, and donors.

☐ I want to be one of the two million people who will join in forty days of prayer and fasting for revival for America, the world, and the fulfillment of the Great Commission.

☐ Please send me *free* information on: ☐ full-time staff, ☐ mid-career change, ☐ part-time associate, ☐ volunteer, ☐ short-term trips, ☐ summer intern, or ☐ employment opportunities with Campus Crusade for Christ.

☐ Please send me *free* information about the other books, booklets, audio cassettes, and videos by Bill and Vonette Bright.

_____
NAME (please print)

_____
ADDRESS

_____
CITY   STATE   ZIP

_____
COUNTRY   E-MAIL

Please check the appropriate box(es), clip, and mail this form to:

Campus Crusade for Christ
375 Highway 74 South, Suite A
Peachtree City, GA 30269

You may also fax your response to (407) 826-2149, or send E-mail to newlifepubs@ccci.org. Visit our website at www.campuscrusade.org